"Caesar Kalinowski is such a wise teacher. Finally, a book on the Christian experience that actually leads its readers toward a new way of living. *Transformed* is a book that every skeptic, seeker, and Christian should read."

— JEN HATMAKER, Author of *7: An Experimental Mutiny Against Excess*

"If there was ever a legitimate time to offer a new pathway for being a Christ-follower, it is now. Thank you, Caesar, for blowing the dust off of the relics of religious life and opening up the window to a God-breathed life."

— HUGH HALTER, Author of *FLESH*, *The Tangible Kingdom*, and *Sacrilege*

"*Transformed: A New Way of Being a Christian* is a brilliant rediscovery by Caesar Kalinowski of what it means to be an apprentice of Jesus! This book is truly transformational by helping us discover our new identity in Christ, a new mission for our lives, and new rhythms for making it happen. Read and be transformed!"

— DAVE FERGUSON, Lead Pastor of Community Christian Church in Naperville, Illinois, and Spiritual Entrepreneur, NewThing

"*Transformed* cuts through the confusion and, at times, disappointment of trying to live 'the Christian life.' If everyone knew the truths that this book illustrates, we would live in a very different world! Caesar's true, powerful stories remind us of the beauty of our birthright, showing us how we can have the life that we were created to live."

— JON TYSON, Pastor of Trinity Grace Church in New York City, co-author of *Rumors of God.*

"In *Transformed*, Caesar Kalinowski challenges us to see that the Christian life is more than a state of mind; it is a way of life that begins with a transformed heart of love. This book will challenge and encourage believers, new and old alike, to live the Christ-like life they are all called to live."

— ED STETZER, Author of *Transformational Groups*, www.edstetzer.com

"I am so glad Caesar Kalinowski has shared with us the insights that have helped to transform so many people in his ministry through the years. These teachings reveal a way of being that opens the door to real living."
— REGGIE MCNEAL, Author of *Missional Communities* and *Get Off Your Donkey!*

"*Transformed* is the fruit of Caesar Kalinowski's many years of faithful labor, serving the poor, sharing Christ with the lost, storytelling, eating, listening to God, and blessing his neighbors. He isn't asking anything of his readers that he's not been prepared to give in his own life. Inspiring!"
— MICHAEL FROST, Morling College, Sydney, and author of *The Road to Missional*

"Caesar's life is his message. I know Caesar well and know that what he communicates in this book has been worked out in the white-hot arena of a life well lived. What he teaches in *Transformed* is true . . . his own life, and the lives of many others, proves it."
ALAN HIRSCH, Author of numerous award-winning books on transformative discipleship, including *Untamed*, *Right Here Right Now*, and *The Faith of Leap*

"As a brilliant storyteller, Caesar Kalinowski has written one of the best books I have read on true biblical discipleship. *Transformed* takes discipleship out of the classroom and places it firmly in our dining room, our workplaces, and our neighborhoods where it belongs."
— BRANDON HATMAKER, Author of *Barefoot Church: Serving the Least in a Consumer Culture*

"This is a book on discipleship unlike any you have ever read. The 'contents' page alone is catnip to the soul."
— LEONARD SWEET, Best-selling author, professor at Drew University and George Fox University, and chief contributor to sermons.com

TRANSFORMED

CAESAR KALINOWSKI

TRANSFORMED

A NEW WAY OF BEING CHRISTIAN

Who We Are and How We Get to Live

ZONDERVAN

Transformed
Copyright © 2013 by Caesar Kalinowski

This title is also available as a Zondervan ebook. Visit www.zondervan.com/ebooks.

Requests for information should be addressed to:

Zondervan, *Grand Rapids, Michigan 49530*

Library of Congress Cataloging-in-Publication Data

Kalinowski, Caesar.
     Transformed : a radical picture of the Christian life : who we are & how we get to live / Caesar Kalinowski. — 1st [edition].
        pages cm
     Includes bibliographical references and index.
     ISBN 978-0-310-33349-4 (softcover)
  1. Christian life. I. Title.
BV4501.3.K355 2014
248.4—dc23   2013018942

The author has used, with their permission, terms and concepts developed by Soma Communities, as noted in the endnotes

Some persons' names and situations have been altered to protect their privacy.

Published in association with the literary agency of WordServe Literary Group, Ltd, Highlands Ranch, Colorado 80130 (www.wordserveliterary.com)

Cover design: Micah Kandros
Cover illustration: iStockphoto®

Printed in the United States of America

14 15 16 17 18 19 /DCI/ 21 20 19 18 17 16 15 14 13 12 11 10 9 8 7 6 5 4 3 2 1

CONTENTS

ACKNOWLEDGMENTS

Now all glory to God, who is able, through his mighty power at work within us, to accomplish infinitely more than we might ask or think. Glory to him in the church and in Christ Jesus through all generations forever and ever!

Ephesians 3:20–21 NLT

I AM THANKFUL to my faithful wife and best friend, Tina, for living out this amazing adventure with me. Your grace is a reminder of God's love every day. To my children, Caesar, Christin, and Justine, thanks for putting up with a dad who is definitely a work in progress. I love you all. I know that you will continue to grow in beauty as your new identity is revealed from glory to glory.

Jeff and Jayne Vanderstelt have remained our friends, partners, and fellow dreamers throughout this entire ride. Much of what is written here was formed in their hearts and through our relationship. I am grateful for you always. I could not have written this without your love and influence in my life. Thanks to Hugh Halter, Matt Smay, and Greg Johnson for the encouragement and faith to go after this.

Special thanks to everyone in Soma Communities everywhere. You have shared your stories and your lives to reveal the love of Christ that has transformed you. This book would not have been possible without all of you.

PART 1

A NEW IDENTITY

I CAN'T REMEMBER A TIME in my life when I felt normal.

I don't mean that I've always been weird, though my wife, kids, and a few of my friends may disagree. What I mean is that from as far back as I can remember, I had a sense that I was destined for something a little out of the ordinary — something bigger, and dare I use the word *special*? Something more important than what I saw and experienced around me.

A bigger purpose.

As a boy, I dreamed of being a superhero. But, alas, I could never get my web shooters to work properly. As a teenager and young man, I thought I'd get my break by becoming a famous rock star, so I played guitar in several bands over a number of years. But soon after I got married, that dream fizzled out.

Go figure!

After I began a relationship with Jesus, putting my hope, trust, and future into his hands, this feeling only intensified. I felt closer to the dream. My heart, for a while, beat a little faster. Was I supposed to go to a foreign land and run an orphanage or hospital? Maybe I should become a male version of Mother Teresa with long hair and a midwestern accent. Did God only use people who were pastors or in full-time ministry to do great things and change the world? And how come my life as a Christian, though it was slowly changing, still looked and felt pretty much like the lives of everyone else in my family and the town I lived in?

A NEW IDENTITY

I found myself a young married father of three small children, still struggling with many of the same sins, attitudes, and relational muck I grew up with. And now I was passing this legacy on to my kids.

Wait. Stop the train!

I finally realized that it wasn't fame or fortune I desired. It was something bigger and much profounder than all of that. I longed to be truly different. To *be* someone else.

I wanted — no, I *needed* — a transformation to occur.

Maybe this is your journey too.

Chapter 1

WHO ARE YOU?

WHEN I WAS A KID, every time we used curse words in my family, my parents would put a mark on a list hanging on the refrigerator. Once a month or so, my father made us take a big ol' lick on a gold-colored bar of Dial soap as a punishment — one lick for every time we cussed. Sometimes those gag-inducing sessions were pretty long. The only silver lining to this story was that my dad, whom we learned most of our curse words from, also took his licks. Fair was fair. I can remember him having to take upwards of fifty or sixty licks on some occasions. That was awesome!

I dreaded those days of soap-licking retribution, though it produced a pretty immediate behavioral modification.

For the moment.

After moving out of my parents' house at age eighteen, I developed a prolific "potty mouth" (to put it nicely). At that time, I had what I thought was the best job in the world — working at a Harley-Davidson dealership. It sort of served as my professional training in the creative and excessive use of foul language, among other things. I became an aficionado, consistently weaving a tapestry of profanity so tight that I became numb to the sheer density and proficiency of my use of foul language. The supposed "discipline" and hoped-for modifications of my soap-licking days hadn't taken root in my life or my use of language.

More on my transformation in that area later.

BUT NOW I'M A CHRISTIAN ...

As Christians we often wonder why we continue to sin in the same old ways, see so little real change in our lives, and possess such a low desire to be "on mission" for God. We generally continue to live our Christian version of the American Dream with a little church attendance thrown in on Sundays and maybe a weekly Bible study when it fits our schedule. If we have stepped up to the level of tithing on our income — well, then we are really getting somewhere.

The sad truth is, we don't experience that big of a change really. Not at the heart level. Not in the nitty-gritty rhythms and stuff of life.

Is this what Jesus came and died on the cross for?

It turns out that for many of us, our "conversion" was really focused on our afterlife (going to heaven and avoiding hell) and has had little effect on our lives in the here and now. What happened to being "new creations"? And why don't we, as the church now, experience life more in line with what we read in Acts 2?

> They devoted themselves to the apostles' teaching and to fellowship, to the breaking of bread and to prayer. Everyone was filled with awe at the many wonders and signs performed by the apostles. All the believers were together and had everything in common. They sold property and possessions to give to anyone who had need. Every day they continued to meet together in the temple courts. They broke bread in their homes and ate together with glad and sincere hearts, prais-

ing God and enjoying the favor of all the people. And the Lord added to their number daily those who were being saved.[1]

Having spent years trying to pastor people asking these same questions, and feeling the ineffectiveness of applying more traditional "spiritual disciplines," I began to wonder how the apostles Paul and Peter, as well as the other disciples, managed to live such transformed lives — lives that were not only *personally* transformed, but that also changed the *world*.

Don't get me wrong here; I am in favor of, and have found great benefit in, many of the more traditional forms of spiritual discipline: time in the Word each day, prayer, keeping a journal, prayer walking, and so on. But as I've learned from reading the writings of mystic and author Henri Nouwen, all of those disciplines are meant to be a means of creating space and time for God to act, for the Spirit to speak to us in intimate ways. The discipline itself is not what changes us — it is God's grace that does.

So perhaps we already have the right pieces to the puzzle, but maybe we've spent years focusing on the wrong things and missing some pretty exciting stuff that could make all the difference in the world.

What's the secret?

WHO ARE YOU?

Several years ago, I spent quite a lot of time going in and out of South Sudan during the decades-long civil war that ravaged the nation and its people. I took part in different missions to deliver much-needed food and lifesaving medicine and to encourage the local Christians as we preached the gospel whenever we could. These experiences were life changing for me in many ways, but one of the biggest things that stuck out — and began to stick *to* me — was how different "church" was in Sudan compared to the life I was living as a Christian, father, and pastor in the United States. It seemed that whenever I was over there in Africa with the Sudanese believers, we *were* the church.

Them and me. Together we were the church.

They didn't have buildings or any resources to "do" church. No elaborate Sunday services with lights and sound systems. *They* just *were* the church. They loved each other, shared what very, very little they had, and literally laid down their lives for the sake of the gospel. And these Christians who owned nothing (no-thing) were filled with joy.

Seriously.

One day while we were distributing food in a refugee camp near the border of Uganda, I met a boy who looked to be about twelve years old.

"Who are you?" I asked him.

His name was James. He was tall and superthin, and just like everyone else in this camp, he had lived through near-starvation and brutal attacks by militant rebels that had decimated his village. I noticed that his left hand and arm were scarred and disfigured, and he had a large patch of hair missing that seemed to have been burned off at some point in the past. I asked our translator if he knew what had happened to the boy. He asked James to tell me his story.

James shared that a few months earlier he and his two brothers were walking with their parents when radical Islamic soldiers hacked his parents to death with machetes right before their eyes — *because they were Christians*. The soldiers then threw him and his two brothers onto a large pile of burning garbage. His brothers died in the fire that day, but James somehow managed to crawl out of the fire and escape with his life.

He then went on to tell me how grateful he was!

I'm not kidding. He was thankful that God had spared his life against all odds that dreadful day, and he knew that he would one day see his family again in heaven and that they were in a safe place now with Jesus. I was blown away. I wept like a baby.

As I spent more time with James and other Christians in the refugee camp that day, I couldn't help but notice they exhibited unbelievable joy. They were the happiest people I had ever been with in my life.

Amid the war, horrible famine, and persecution they suffered on a daily basis, these brothers and sisters in Christ were filled with a sense of peace and joy that I had never personally experienced. Shouldn't I, with all of my American health, wealth, and comfort be happier and more grateful than them?

I remember crying out to God, saying, "I would trade everything I have to experience the joy they find in you!"

And God replied, *Then do.*

Ouch. It sort of felt like what Jesus had to say to the rich young ruler in Matthew 19. Paraphrasing, here's the story:

> A young man came up to Jesus and asked, "What good things must I do to get into the kingdom?"
> Jesus replied, "God is the only one who is good. Follow his commandments."
> The man said, "I have obeyed his commands — what else must I do?"
> "Go sell everything you have and give the money to the poor, and you will have heavenly treasures. Then come and follow me."[2]

Did I need to get rid of all of my personal (and my family's) possessions in order to find true joy and purpose in my Christian life? Did I need to move to Africa to really *be* the church?

The point of this story Jesus told wasn't to get us all to go and sell our stuff; it was for us to see where our true treasure, hope, and delight are found. Do we find our happiness, security, and purpose in our stuff and from what we *do* — or in who we *are* because of who he is?

IT'S ALL ABOUT JESUS

James and the other Sudanese Christians I spent time with had no possessions, no country, no homes, and in some cases, no earthly families — nothing left to put their hope in. But they had found the only thing that truly satisfies the human heart: Jesus. They didn't have or need material possessions to be happy, and there was nothing profound for them to do.

They had found their very life — their identity and purpose — in Jesus.

As Christians they (and we) are a part of a family whose Father is God himself. Jesus is our Brother. And we have been sent by the Spirit on a life-altering mission to see more and more people come to know Jesus and find eternal life and the peace he offers.

It is Jesus who pursues, secures, and maintains our position in the family of God. He died that we might be restored to a right relationship with his Father, back into the family we were originally created to be a part of. Jesus, our Servant King, gave us his indwelling Spirit and sent us out on his mission.

It's all about Jesus.

The Bible teaches that if we are in Christ, we have become part of a family of missionary servants, sent as disciples who make disciples.[3]

This is who we are. This is our new *identity*. This is the secret.

The more we understand and believe this to be true, the more our lives will be transformed — and the more peace, joy, and purpose we will find in life.

So who are *you*?

BAPTIZED INTO THIS NEW IDENTITY

If you've ever been baptized or witnessed a baptismal ceremony, you've seen and heard Jesus' answer to that question. But maybe you missed it. In Matthew 28:19, he lays out the entire picture and command for us this way: "Therefore go and make disciples of all nations, baptizing them in the name of the Father and of the Son and of the Holy Spirit." There it is: our identity and mission as the church and the means to accomplish it.

Our baptism is not some magic, saving spell or just a culturally ancient ritual; we are baptized, soaked, given a new identity within a new community — the church.

In the *name of* the Father and the *name of* the Son and the *name of* the Holy Spirit — this constitutes a profound identity statement about who we are now. Let's take a quick look at each of these.

GOD IS OUR DADDY

Our name has everything to do with whose family we belong to. In the past, if your last name was Johnson, you may have had a father named John, and if you were his son — well, you get the picture. Maybe as Christians we should all have the last name Godson, for God is our Father. The living God of the universe is the Daddy (Abba)[4] of the church, and we are his children.

"Both the one who makes people holy and those who are made holy are of the same family. So Jesus is not ashamed to call them brothers and sisters."[5] Jesus calls us his brothers and sisters, which points to the reality that the church is a family. It is part of our transformed identity, and we'll look deeply into how our family identity shapes the church in chapter 3.

Unlike our human fathers, God is the consistently patient Father. He is the ultimate provider. He is a perfectly caring and protective Father. Regardless of how good of a dad we had growing up, he was flawed and imperfect. But not our heavenly Father. He'll never yell (or curse) at us and never leave or abandon us. He will never harm or abuse us. We have an eternal and never-changing, loving Father, and we are his family on this earth.

SAVED TO SERVE

We have entered into a relationship with Jesus that defines our identity. He is not only our Brother; he is also our King. And we are now his servants who serve others as a way of life, following Jesus' ultimate example on the cross. Being a servant is a part of our renewed identity. In fact, Jesus reminds his followers of their new reality: "Whoever wants to be first must be your slave — just as the Son of Man did not come to be served, but to serve, and to give his life as a ransom for many."[6]

When Jesus washed his disciples' feet just days before his death, he showed them a clear picture of who he was and who he was making them to be. At first, Peter, who often spoke before thinking, declared that he would never allow Jesus to wash his feet. But Jesus told his disciples, "Very truly I tell you, no servant is greater than his master, nor is a messenger greater than the one who sent him."[7]

When I was a new believer, an older "brother" befriended me and spent time teaching me about our identity as a servant. Johnnie became a lifelong mentor and friend of mine as he listened to me; modeled Christlike behavior for me; and prayed, ate meals, and laughed (a lot) with me. One thing I noticed about Johnnie was that he *always* opened the door for his wife, Ruth. He would practically kill himself to beat her around the car to get that door open for her. He also honored her by seating her at the dinner table. I don't think Ruth has pulled out her own chair to sit down in thirty years!

Well, maybe this Johnnie is just a nice guy, you might be thinking. But then I noticed something that really messed with me and forever changed my experience in public bathrooms.

Whenever Johnnie and I were in a restroom at the same time, I often saw him picking up any discarded paper towels or toilet paper that was accidentally or carelessly left on the floor. He would always pick it up and throw it away before washing up and leaving. This kind of grossed me out, and (much like the apostle Peter) I thought to myself, *I would never do that — that is crazy!* When I asked Johnnie why he did it, he said, "That is what a servant does. He cleans up the mess that others make in life — just like Jesus did for us."

Boom. And just like that, I have been picking up runaway paper products in bathrooms ever since.

Thanks, Johnnie!

Thanks, Jesus.

What begins to happen when we believe our identity as a servant, and when we grasp the degree to which we have been served by Jesus, is that we naturally begin to serve. Because this is who we are, serving becomes an act of worship and an immediate display of what Jesus is like. Opportunities — big and small — to live as servants are all around us every day. We'll spend a lot more time looking at this in chapter 5.

COME AND SEE OR GO AND MAKE?

Throughout the Bible, the Holy Spirit is the sending agent of the church. He empowered Jesus while on earth, he guided and comforted the early church, and his indwelling presence transforms our identity into "sent ones," literally *missionaries.*

When I was a boy growing up in the Midwest, our church building had a big map of the world in the lobby with pins marking places where we supported "missionaries." There were also pictures of these missionaries, who were usually dressed in outdated clothing and looked rather sad. Every once in a while, one of these missionaries would come and visit on a Sunday and tell us stories from "the field" and show us pictures of skinny, dirty children with flies on their eyes and lips. Yuck. Then the pastor would pass the offering baskets to take up a special offering for them. Twice.

We were taught that these people in the photographs, who always worked and served in faraway lands, were the missionaries. They never told us what the Bible teaches: *all* Christians are missionaries. After his resurrection, Jesus appeared to his disciples behind locked doors and commissioned them: "'Peace be with you! As the Father has sent me, I am sending you.' And with that he breathed on them and said, 'Receive the Holy Spirit.' "[8]

The church is not a building; the church is people. Always has been. I am not sure how we came to refer to the buildings that we often gather in on Sunday as "the church," but it is some pretty bad theology. In my community, we often, somewhat jokingly, correct one another when someone says, "I'll see you at church on Sunday." We respond, "You can't *go* to church; you *are* the church!"

The church has always been a "sent" people. Jesus never intended that we primarily find our Christian life and expression through a one- to two-hour service once a week inside a building. We have the other six days and twenty-two hours each week to live out our identity as his missionary family. Jesus' command to *"go* and make disciples" was not a suggestion.

And Jesus didn't say, "Ask people to *come* and see." He always intended — and his life is our example — that we would incarnate (give bodily form to) his mission out in the world, neighborhood, offices, gyms, parks, and so on to show what he is like and to share the gospel by both our life's display and our words. Regardless of how God decides to route our paychecks, whether through a business or through a church, we are all full-time, paid missionaries.

The idea of all believers being missionaries did not start with Jesus or the apostles. This missionary identity is part of who our Father God is and has always been. In Genesis 3 we read the sad story of Adam and Eve's distrust of God and rebellion and the first human sin. Watch what happens right after Eve and Adam eat the forbidden fruit:

> Then the man and his wife heard the sound of the LORD God as he was walking in the garden in the cool of the day, and they hid from the LORD God among the trees of the garden. But the LORD God called to the man, "Where are you?"[9]

As soon as the first humans sinned against God in disobedience, God set out on the first recorded missionary journey looking for his beloved children. "Where are you?" he called out. Immediately after we sinned, God set out on a rescue mission. That is what he is like. Jesus is a lot like his Dad, and we were originally created in his image — to be like him too.[10]

OUR NEW LITTLE SISTER

A few years ago I received a phone call from a woman I did not know, asking me if I would be willing to meet with her daughter, Jody. She shared with me that Jody was suffering from major clinical depression, was a drug user, and had recently attempted suicide. I was a little surprised that someone in Jody's situation would want to meet with me, presumably to talk about spiritual things, but I agreed to meet with her if she was up for it.

We met at a local café. Jody was a highly tattooed twentysomething, very thin, and perpetually shaking from the cocktail of drugs she took for her depression, on top of alcohol abuse. The dark circles under her eyes added to her hollow look. I remember that she seemed like a scared puppy who had been beaten by a horrible master. But when I asked her to tell me her story, immediately I could see that she was amazingly smart, articulate, and ready to talk.

Jody told me she had grown up in a house with a mother who saw a pretty steady string of men who came in and out of their lives. Sex and drugs were always around for her both to see and to participate in from a very early age. Her mother also suffered from clinical depression and was the one who had suggested Jody start taking many of the same drugs she was on. Two years earlier, Jody found out she had cancer. Her boyfriend at the time, Nick, immediately abandoned her because he "could not deal with this cancer stuff." She had recovered (miraculously) from the cancer, alone, and had then reunited with Nick, with whom she was currently living. A week previous to our visit, she found out she was pregnant, and Nick promptly moved out again, saying he could not handle that either. She was contemplating ending her life.

In the weeks and months that followed, the Holy Spirit carefully guided my wife and I, along with our missional community, to pursue Jody. He sent us on an extended rescue mission. At first, even though she said she wanted our help, she stopped answering phone calls. I had to drive over to her apartment in order to talk with her. She didn't have a car, so we began to serve Jody by giving her rides to work or to doctor's appointments. Eventually we even picked her up to come celebrate, eat, and experience God with our church community on Sunday mornings. She found peace being with this family and had a desire to know God and "get her life straightened out."

She could no longer afford to keep her apartment since she was now living alone, so our missional community collectively paid $1,800 to get her out of the lease on the apartment and helped move her and her dog into the home of another couple in our community. Jody slowly stopped taking all of the medications that were supposed to help her depression and found that she was healthier, happier, and more clearheaded without them. Her shaking stopped and she became physically healthy for the first time in years as the baby inside of her grew and grew. Her faith in Jesus also grew as she began to believe that he loved her dearly and would never abandon her or forget about her. He *could* deal with her stuff. She had seen and experienced his love from our community (his family), and it forever changed her life.

It was there with us, protected and cared for, that Jody put her faith in Jesus. She became a child of God, our sister, and a new mother that year. She was part of the family.

Living as a family of missionary servants is what it means to be a disciple of Jesus. This is our new identity. We are this way because God is this way. Our new identity is not based on what we *do*; it is found in who we *are*.

The way of the world is that we do things (perform, serve, work, etc.) to have value in the eyes of our family, friends, parents, spouse, siblings, boss, pastor, and others. If we do a good enough job and are perceived as valuable, people will want us around. Out of this activity, we often form our identity. What we *do* has led to who we *are* — or at least we think it has. But this way of living is terribly dangerous, for it goes against how God sees us, and eventually it crushes us.

Don't believe the *do* = *be* lies anymore.

THINGS TO THINK ABOUT

How would your life change if you lived solely out of your identity in Christ, as an image bearer of God?

How would your relationships change if you viewed and treated others based on their identity as image bearers of God?

How would our lives, our families, and churches change if we believed our new identity and began to live like a family of missionary servants?

How would others in the world perceive us if we lived this way?

Chapter 2

A NEW WAY OF BEING

IF YOU HAPPEN to be asking yourself why you are still reading a book by a confessed foul-mouthed pastor, let me tell you the rest of that story. When I truly put my trust in Jesus, a transformation began to take place. My vulgar vocabulary, spoken mostly out of habit, actually started to taste foul in my mouth. No one told me to stop swearing; none of my new friends in the church said, "You know, Christians shouldn't talk like that!" But I had a strong, growing feeling inside that that is not who Jesus is — that it was not who *I* was anymore. I felt that it didn't please my heavenly Father, and I knew I wouldn't talk that way if I could see him there next to me.

Almost overnight my words changed. My heart no longer desired or needed to speak that way as the Holy Spirit gave me new and better ways to communicate. My new identity began to transform my words.

Out of the overflow of the heart, the mouth speaks.

SOME MORE GOOD NEWS

So if what we've been talking about so far is true, how does God now view us? Are there strings attached to this new relationship and identity? At times I can flip back and forth between resting and wrestling with this reality.

We must begin to believe who God says we are.

> There were seasons early on when I believed: I have been changed into a new creature. I am fused with Jesus. He loves me and enjoys me all the time. He is maturing me in his way, in his time. I can trust and receive love. Most of the rest of my time I've believed: I changed in a legal sense, but not really. He is usually disappointed with me. He expects me to at least try to fix myself. I can't be trusted or trust anyone else.[1]

When you pray (talk with God), do you spend most of your time thinking about and apologizing for sins and messed-up stuff in your life? Do you feel, *If I only sinned a little less or worked for God a little more, he would finally be pleased with me*? Or do you more often simply enjoy being with God in his presence? Our good Father is waiting each day to say, *I love you. I love spending time with you; you bring me great joy!*

Do you believe that? Because if God has a refrigerator, your picture is on it!

For years I believed the bumper sticker theology that told me I was a "saved sinner" instead of the truth that I am now a saint (member of God's family) who still sins. The reason we continue to rebel against God and sin is that we have not fully trusted in his grace and are not living out of our new identity — that we are who we are because of what Jesus did. The Bible says we really are new people, completely righteous. Jesus became sin so we might be made righteous; he didn't become theoretical sin. He actually became real sin (our sin) in every possible way that sin can be sin. And if the corollary holds, then we didn't become righteousness theoretically. We became real righteousness in every possible way that righteousness can be righteousness.[2] When you read that Jesus "became sin," think of it this way: God charged all of our sins to Jesus' account and credited his perfect life and righteousness to our side of the bill.

My grasp of this concept has been helped by understanding the word *righteousness* as right-use-ness. What is the right-use-ness of a pencil? To write things. What is the right-use-ness of a hammer? To pound nails.

What is our right-use-ness? It is to live out our new identity, trusting God and believing what he says to be true of us. This is how Jesus lived. We are now the righteousness of Christ,[3] and the motivation of a righteous heart is no longer toward sin — it is toward love. Why? Because we have been so extravagantly loved ourselves. The same way and to the same extent that the Father loves Jesus, he also loves us — and Jesus loves us to the same extent that he has been loved by the Father. "As the Father has loved me, so have I loved you. Now remain in my love."[4]

God's love transforms us. It protects us. It perfects us.

Receiving and giving God's love is what we were created to experience. It is what our human hearts have always desired. And as crazy as this may sound, God's ongoing goal is not to change us. He already has. His goal is to mature us, to empower us to establish trusting relationships with him in all areas of our lives.

When I trust I am a new creation through the work of Jesus on the cross, I begin to live life closer to God, a life of fullness and peace. I live freer from the power of sin and am free to love without reservation. I learn to believe that all God's power, love, truth, and righteousness already exist in me right now. Even on my worst day.[5] I begin to live out my new, restored identity.

BABY STEPS ON STEROIDS

But the good news doesn't end there. We are not made new creations, given a new identity, and then shoved out the door and told to go and live out this new life in our own strength, power, and wisdom. God does not expect us, all of a sudden, to become perfect super-Christians — always wise, gentle, and loving overnight. The Bible compares this new life to taking a walk, one step at a time, each new area of trust in God connected to the next, as God matures us on a journey in the footsteps of Jesus. As we believe more and more deeply what is now true of us in Christ, we experience that we have been made new inside and out. It's God's work, not ours!

> It is God who enables us, along with you, to stand firm for Christ. He has commissioned us, and he has identified us as his own by placing the Holy Spirit in our hearts as the first installment that guarantees everything he has promised us.[6]

We are not filled with an emotional feeling, a hunch, or more zing. We are filled with a *person*.

For most of my early life as a Christian, I never picked up that Jesus' earthly ministry was guided completely by the Holy Spirit. I had always thought, *Well, Jesus is both God and man, so he knows what's up and just naturally does everything perfectly.*

Well, sort of.

It's true that Jesus is both God and man, and that he lived his life without ever sinning. But as a human, like you and me, he fully submitted to and was guided by the Spirit. His life is a picture of the perfect work of the Holy Spirit in man.

> Jesus was born by the work of the Spirit (Luke 1:35).
> Jesus was led by the Spirit to suffer temptation and come
>   out spotless (Luke 4:1–2).

Jesus was empowered by the Spirit to do the ministry he
did (Matt. 12:28; Acts 10:38).

Jesus was full of wisdom and knowledge by the Holy Spirit
(Isa. 11:2–3).

Jesus spoke only the words given him by the Spirit (John
3:34; 8:28).

Jesus was raised from the dead by the power of the Spirit
(Rom. 8:11).

Wouldn't it be great if we had this same Spirit living inside of us,
guiding, empowering, and giving us words to say (or not say)?

Oh, wait! We do.

> The Spirit of God, who raised Jesus from the dead, lives in
> you. And just as God raised Christ Jesus from the dead, he
> will give life to your mortal bodies by this same Spirit living
> within you.[7]

The same power that guided Jesus' life and raised him from the
dead now lives in us. That's pretty powerful!

So I am going to go out on a limb here and suggest that if the
Spirit was powerful enough to raise Jesus, and if the very same
Spirit now lives in and empowers us, we will have enough strength
to overcome our old bad temper, a hard day at work, disobedient
kids, an argument with our spouse, hurts and shattered dreams,
lack of love for the lost, and on and on. See what I mean?

THE POWER'S ON

Last year, during a particularly busy time in my life when I was
feeling increasingly exhausted, I started to pray, asking the Spirit
for strength to get through the day. Usually, around 7:00 or 8:00
p.m., when faced with one more meeting, phone call, or invitation
to hang out in community, my personal desire was to curl up on

the couch and just vegetate in front of the television before going to bed. But I noticed that if I prayed to the Spirit for strength, and for a good attitude to go along with it, he was always faithful to give me what I needed to finish the day and that "one last thing" I needed to do.

Then it dawned on me. *Duh! Why do I wait until the end of my day, the end of my strength — the end of my rope — to ask the Spirit for strength? Why not do that first thing in the morning when I wake up?*

So I started asking, and guess what happened? My day *started* in his strength and grace and continued on this way. Not perfectly, because sometimes I would forget to ask and receive. But things began to change because of this. God began to cultivate in me a moment-by-moment dependency on the Spirit that continues to grow today. It turns out that the old way of trying to live my life — doing many "good things" in my own strength — was actually sinful.

In the Old Testament, the Israelites saw God's strength, power, and provision over and over again but still returned to worshiping false idols (anything that people trust in that is not God). Even "good things" like giving money to the poor or serving widows and performing acts of worship were done in their own strength and faith in their abilities. The prophet Isaiah confessed, "All of us have become like one who is unclean, and all our righteous acts are like filthy rags."[8]

Isaiah's mention of "filthy rags" is a reference to dirty menstrual cloths. Today we call them tampons. What the prophet Isaiah was reminding them, and us, is that even our ministry, worship, and hard work — when it is not dependent on faith in God and his strength — is really just a big stack of used tampons piled up before him.

None of us wants that!

FRUIT INSPECTION

We see time and again in the New Testament that the early believers did nothing outside the direction and strength of the Holy Spirit.[9] But in Galatians 5:13–26 we are given a picture of one group of young Christians who tried to live this new Good News life in their own strength. The writer, the apostle Paul, calls this our old "sinful nature." In my summary of what Paul says here, notice the two choices we seem to have:

> As God's children we've been called to live in freedom. So let's turn control of our lives over to the Holy Spirit to lead and guide us. Then we won't be driven by our selfishness and personal preferences in the moment. The sinful nature, conditioned from childhood, wants things its own way, but the Spirit gives us desires that are just the opposite. You can't have it both ways! It's pretty clear what happens when we allow our old sinful nature to take charge — just look at the world today: Sex lives that are mixed up, messed up, and self-focused. Man-made little "gods" that are served in vain. Selfish anger mixed up with control issues that lead to fighting, backstabbing, and jealousy. All kinds of drunken parties and gross addictions. I could keep on going. But what happens when we live new, Spirit-transformed lives? We'll be like a superproductive orchard overflowing with the sweet fruits of abundant, selfless love. We'll have serenity — at times even joy — in the storms of life. We'll have patience for things and people that are different than us, and a gentle, kind commitment to let God be God in others' lives.

I think we can all agree that the second list, found in Galatians 5:22–23 — the fruit of the Spirit, which includes love, joy, peace, forbearance, kindness, goodness, faithfulness, gentleness, and self-control — looks a whole lot better than the first list, the acts of the flesh, found in verses 19–21. But I have often wondered why I so often return to trying to live this new life using my own strength and old ways of thinking. It is like a bad habit that I cannot shake.

It all stems back, again, to believing what God says to be true of us and allowing the Spirit to realign our motivation, priorities, and actions with the truth.

> Nature provides many examples of this incredible discrepancy between who we appear to be and who we truly are. Consider the caterpillar. If we brought a caterpillar to a biologist and asked him to analyze it and describe its DNA, he would tell us, "I know this looks like a caterpillar to you. But scientifically, according to every test, including DNA, this is fully and completely a butterfly." Wow! God has wired into a creature looking nothing like a butterfly a perfectly complete butterfly identity. And because the caterpillar is a butterfly in essence, it will one day display the behavior and attributes of a butterfly. The caterpillar matures into what is already true about it.[10]

To try and muster up this new life is not our job; it is the work of the Holy Spirit. We can no more effectively live out this new identity than we can save our self from sin and death.

God saved us. God transformed us. God empowers our new identity.

THE JOURNEY AHEAD

This book will not be theoretical, propositional, and without practical outworking, for our identity always leads to how we live our lives. God's loving nature always leads him to *express* his love. His love for us, in turn, leads us to express love to others, showing the world what he is like. Just as we saw that our "good works" are like filthy rags when done apart from faith, so our faith and belief lead us to new ways of living; otherwise, they are useless and dead.

> What good is it, dear brothers and sisters, if you say you have faith but don't show it by your actions? Can that kind of faith save anyone? Suppose you see a brother or sister who has

no food or clothing, and you say, "Good-bye and have a good day; stay warm and eat well" — but then you don't give that person any food or clothing. What good does that do? So you see, faith by itself isn't enough. Unless it produces good deeds, it is dead and useless.[11]

We get a great picture of this in a story from Jesus' own life. His cousin, known as John the Baptist, was in prison (and soon to die) because John offended Herod when he challenged the king's relationship with his sister-in-law, whom Herod had taken as his wife. Things weren't really going that well for John, and he was beginning to wonder if he should look elsewhere for hope. So John sent his friends to ask Jesus if he was "the One," the hoped-for Messiah, or if they should wait for another.

Jesus answered John's messengers with what I call his kingdom job description: "Go back and report to John what you have seen and heard: The blind receive sight, the lame walk, those who have leprosy are cleansed, the deaf hear, the dead are raised, and the good news is proclaimed to the poor."[12]

And I wonder if the world today, your friends and mine — our neighbors — are asking, "Are you the ones we've been waiting for, or should we expect something else? My life stinks over here, and I was really expecting a different kind of Christian or church to show up and help us put things right. Is this it?"

Do we publicly bear the image that Jesus bore? Do we do the things Jesus did? Could we answer the way he answered? And would we answer from who we are or what we did — or didn't — do? Would we be convinced by our own answers?

"Well, um, we have three services on Sunday now with a new and improved children's ministry wing. Our youth group is the biggest in the county. . . ."

"Yeah, but my boyfriend left me alone and pregnant, and I already have two kids from my first failed marriage. I also just found out that my job is being outsourced to another state, and I am scared out of my mind. Are you the ones who can help ... or should I look for someone else?"

And then we ask ourselves, *How would a family of missionary servants respond to this?*

Did John and his followers miss that Jesus was the Messiah because he hid who he was from them? Was John not standing there in the Jordan River with water up to his waist after baptizing Jesus, and did he not hear the Father's voice from heaven declare, "This is my Son"?

Jesus went on and healed and fed people and proclaimed the good news of the kingdom of God out of who he was. His identity was working itself out publicly in front of them, proving who his Father had declared him to be. When asked about himself, Jesus pointed them to the evidence of his identity being lived out in his life.

In our case, most people don't miss who we are as the church because they have not heard what we say or preach to (at) them; they miss who we are because they have seen little to no evidence that we are the transformed people of Jesus. We have not begun to live out of what is now true for us.

WHO ... ME?

Picture this: When you were born, some long-lost uncle placed a billion dollars into a bank account under your name. He planned to give it to you when you became an adult, but on the way home from the bank that day, he was killed in an accident, and all records of that money — your money — were lost forever. Unbeknownst to you, the deposit has now sat in that bank account accruing interest for twenty, thirty, forty years, or more. With interest, this treasure has grown to be worth a zillion dollars.

A NEW WAY OF BEING

One day, miraculously, evidence is finally found proving whose money this is that has been sitting in the bank all these years. You can hardly believe it's true even after being told this mind-blowing news and shown the proof.

You've never known it was there, and you have lived your life, like a lot of people, working hard to make ends meet. At times you have even done a few things to get by that you were not all that proud of. How different would your life be if you had only known about this amazing inheritance that was yours all along?

Now imagine that this inheritance multiplied in unfathomable ways and has been given to you, because this is what is now true for you as a child of God. You have become coheir of *all things* in the world with Jesus. God's own Spirit has come to live in you and love you through every step of your life from here on out. It seems too good to be true.

But it is true.

I have spent the last eight years as part of a church family, Soma Communities, in Tacoma, Washington, that is learning to live out our new identity in all the normal, everyday rhythms of life. Families, single moms, students, dockworkers, dentists, homeless people, teens, kids — even pastors — are all stumbling forward in the arms of grace and experiencing something we all dreamed of but never before thought possible this side of the Bible.

As we continue on, we'll look deeply into our new identity and how it begins to shape every aspect and priority of our lives. We'll see how this sets us free from performance-driven motives and guilt, leading us into daily rhythms of life where we are often already being and doing what we have been saved to be and do.

THINGS TO THINK ABOUT

How would your prayers to God change if you fully believed that he was your Daddy and you were his dearly loved child?

How would your relationship with God change if you lived before him as a completely forgiven saint who still occasionally sins? (God is not surprised by your sin.)

How would your relationships change if you were to see others as God sees them?

How would others perceive what our Father and Jesus are like if we began to live out of our identity in the strength and guidance of the Holy Spirit?

PART 2

IDENTITY:
WHO WE ARE

CAN YOU IMAGINE PERFORMING as a one-person high-flying trapeze act? There you are, swinging back and forth high above the crowds, picking up incredible height and speed, and then *whoosh*! Off into the air you fly. You do a double — no, a triple! — somersault and some freaky midair spin before being caught by ... no one.

It doesn't work, does it?

The Lone Ranger has Tonto. Batman has Robin, the Boy Wonder. Sherlock Holmes is nothing without Dr. Watson. Even Han Solo has Chewbacca to watch his back! All great exploits happen with a little help from our friends.

I've always wondered why as Christians we seem to think our spiritual life is ultimately something to be lived as a solo, private exercise? Can you hear it in the ways we talk about our faith?

"I made a personal decision for Christ...."
"In my personal relationship with God ..."
"In my personal prayer life ..."

Partly this comes from believing in a gospel that is primarily focused on — well, *me*.

Me getting saved.
Me getting forgiven.
Me finding peace.
Me avoiding hell.

Me going to heaven.
Me, my, mine.

Now, while it is certainly true that we can and should have a deep, intimate relationship with God, one in which we know him personally, the Christian life was never meant to be *private*, lived in isolation, or reduced to a couple of hours on Sunday, sitting among other believers in silence. We were created to live out our identity as the family of God, together with and for each other — and then ultimately live outward as we invite others into this forever-family.

Our transformed existence comes from our God, who exists as three-in-one: Father, Son, and Holy Spirit. God exists in community, and we were created in such a way that we reflect this eternal, loving community. This new identity is lived both individually and collectively — as the church.

As we move on, we will look closely — and more specifically — at what this new identity looks like *in community*, living together as a family of missionary servants sent as disciples who make disciples in everyday life. Each of the four key expressions of our identity — families, missionaries, servants, disciples — will be more fully explored and fleshed out as I share stories and illustrations from my life lived as part of a missional community.

You'll notice that each of these four expressions will overlap and blend together as we go along. This is because they are not four separate identities; rather, they are all part of our one true identity in Christ.

Chapter 3

FAMILY

*We are now children of God, brothers and sisters
living and caring for each other as a family.*

EVERY YEAR since my kids were little, our family has watched the movie *A Christmas Story* together on Christmas Eve. We go early to our Christmas Eve service then race home, change into our pajamas (this is a very important step), and pop massive amounts of popcorn. We lie piled up together on the couch or on blankets strewn around the floor and pretty much recite every line of the movie as it happens. Watching this midwestern family going through their holiday traditions — now a part of ours — never gets old.

In the movie, a young boy, Ralphie, who is growing up in 1940s Indiana, attempts to convince his parents, teachers, and even Santa that he *needs* "an official Red Ryder, carbine action, two-hundred-shot range model air rifle" for Christmas! Humorously, he is consistently met with the objection, "You'll shoot your eye out!"

Of course the climax of the movie — and it never gets old — is when all the presents have seemingly been opened on Christmas morning, and Ralphie's constantly cranky father, who really loves and serves his family, pulls one last hidden box from behind the desk next to the family Christmas tree. As Ralphie shreds through the wrapping, he discovers the hoped-for Red Ryder BB gun! I love this part because it reminds me of the gun my own father got me for Christmas one year.

My mother was not very happy either.

As our community in Tacoma grew, we started inviting others to join us for this tradition. A few years back, we had more than forty friends — some believers and some not yet, the young, the old, the conservative, and the massively tattooed — join us on Christmas Eve.

Pajamas were mandatory, of course.

We could barely fit into the house together and had to set up two TVs in different rooms. What a blast! Now our family tradition has become their tradition, and these friends and neighbors are becoming our family.

What I have learned from this tradition and others in my life is that *sharing* them is the key. It isn't this particular movie that is so awesome (though it kind of is); rather, it is whom we participate in it with that is so special. We choose to be together and hang our shared memories, hopes, and dreams on doing this again and again. Our common need is not the movie experience in pajamas every year — it is one another. Together we form a picture of diversity and acceptance that is uncommon today. We are richer, more diverse, and more wonderful together than we are without one another.

Together we are a better picture of what God is like.

A FAMILY RESEMBLANCE

God has always desired a people — an earthly family — who would live in such a way that the world would see and know what he is truly like. This was his hope for the people of Israel. He walked with them for thousands of years, providing for their needs, showing them his love and protection, and sending them out to do the same with and for others.

But the people rejected God and chose to live only for themselves, treating the other nations as outsiders. Separating themselves from the "unclean," they chose to live primarily with those who were most like them, rejecting those they did not want to associate with. They were more concerned with preserving *their image* than God's, focusing more on their priorities than on God's glory.

Now the church is God's family, his "Plan A" for loving the world. Because we have been so radically and sacrificially loved as his children, it is our privilege to proactively, generously care for the needs of one another both physically and spiritually. This life we now live as God's family is not a burden; it is a privilege. It is not that we *have* to live this way. We *get* to. Sharing life together, centered on the gospel, is the closest thing this side of heaven to walking with Jesus in the flesh. And as we do, we show the world the heart of our heavenly Daddy.

> The irony is that while God doesn't need us but still wants us, we desperately need God but don't really want him most of the time. He treasures us ... and we wonder, indifferently, how much we have to do for him to get by.[1]

Part of the goal of a healthy family is to pass on its patterns from parent to child, from older sibling to younger sibling, to prepare new humans to inhabit the world in ways that are healthy and productive and that carry on the family's unique traditions. The book of Proverbs encourages parents to "start children off in the way they should go,"[2] for kids indeed grow up and copy their parents (for good and for bad); in the same way, we copy our heavenly Dad and Brother.

God has created his church as a family full of siblings (and parents) to shape us, guide us, protect us, and discipline us.

BECOMING FAMILY

Greg is a brother of mine in community who has really come full circle in his life and understanding of what it means to be God's family on mission. He first found our community, and a new relationship with Jesus, through playing cards in a series of friendly Texas Hold'em games that some of our guys hosted. Greg found a family and a place to get his questions answered as he began a new life in Christ.

Playing poker for Jesus! Go figure.

A few years later, Greg began helping to lead our sister organization, Network Tacoma, which owns and manages thirty-four units of transitional housing in and around Tacoma, helping homeless families get off the street. He has worked hard to help those who live in our apartments build relationships within our missional communities in Soma. He has always believed that these dear people need more than a roof over their head; they need a family of friends who will serve them and walk with them through the hardest times of their lives, showing them the gospel in action.

One of the very first families Greg and his wife, Mary, began to invite into their lives was a sixteen-year-old girl named Kirstan and her widowed mother, Julianna. They had a pretty rough story. Their family had suffered from multigenerational drug abuse, addiction, and violence. Kirstan's dad spent years in and out of jail while her mom was a functional alcoholic. At one point, she ate nothing but meals from Jack in the Box for six months because it was the only thing she could walk to from the low-cost motel the family was living in at the time. Her mom would slap down some cash on the table and leave for a few days, telling Kirstan and her sister to "take care of stuff." A few months before Greg met them, Kirstan's dad had committed suicide by hanging himself in her grandparents' garage — a very, very sad story. Eventually homeless, and unsure what to do, the family wandered into our offices.

FAMILY

Kirstan looked a little like a Goth, dressed all in black with long, fortress-like bangs covering most of her expressionless face. She failed the necessary drug screening that was required to get into an apartment, but showing them grace, Greg decided to take a chance on Kirstan and Julianna, and moved them into one of our two-bedroom units.

Greg and Mary started praying and looking for ways to get Kirstan and Julianna beyond the meeting table at the housing offices and to their dinner table at home. It took three to four months and several invitations before Kirstan and her mom finally reluctantly accepted.

That first evening Kirstan was very quiet and her mom ate as fast as she could so they could leave to go watch *American Idol*. They chitchatted through dinner, and for some reason Julianna expressed a desire to be a part of a church. Weird. They told her about the weekly dinners they had with some of their friends on Thursday nights and invited Julianna and Kirstan to join them. The very next week, they started coming to have dinner with the missional community. That was four years ago, and they've never stopped coming. For the first few months, they were pretty much just observers — quiet, feeling out relationships, but not saying much or divulging their personal life situations with the group.

Though Julianna was a servant who loved to bring food, she was a little scared of being vulnerable with others, which was totally understandable! But with time and many interactions, Kirstan and her mom realized that this crazy group of Jesus people were more interested in them being part of their family than getting them to start "going to church," or to stop doing this or that in their lives. They began to lean into relationships a little more. Family was still scary — you could get hurt — but they were beginning to trust.

They were starting to believe a new story.

At one of these Thursday night "family" dinners, Julianna really opened up for the first time, talking about how hurt and how angry she was at her husband for killing himself, for leaving them alone, for hurting her daughters. She was crying as she shared, and for the first time, Kirstan moved from her safe corner, where she usually sat, into the circle of friends to comfort her mom. She never left the circle after that. Full of great insights and questions, she had a lot to offer the group. God, faith, and family were beginning to become real to her.

At one point, Kirstan mentioned that she was sorry she had dropped out of high school. One of the young fathers in the group asked her what was keeping her from going back and finishing. With a puzzled look on her face, she said, "I'm not sure really."

Everyone rallied around her and helped pay for her to get a GED (high school equivalency diploma). She was very much "big-brothered" by the community through the process. Once all of the pieces were in place, Kirstan did everything she needed to do to graduate. She was amazing!

A few months later, at the age of seventeen, Kirstan completed the courses and walked the stage in cap and gown to receive her diploma. What a day! God rewrote her story from being a homeless dropout to getting her diploma and graduating a year before everyone else! Greg and others from her missional community went to the ceremony, and they have a picture of her that day, hair long and flowing under her tasseled graduation cap. She is smiling, positively glowing, and her mom is in the picture, so proud and happy.

What a contrast this was from when Julianna and Kirstan first walked into our offices looking for any help they could find. Kirstan's bangs were long then, covering her eyes and most of her face. Her mom's face was swollen from crying, wondering where her kids were going to sleep that night. What a change. What good news, for them and for us, as we saw grace, restoration, trust, and hope in action — in the flesh. A true picture of the gospel.

In so many ways, this is a story that belongs to all of us. None of us has a perfect family or has been the perfect son, daughter, mother, father, sister, or brother. We have all, at times, lived for our own "glory" and tried to manage life and relationships to suit our own personal comfort and liking. Or perhaps we have been sinned against and felt abandoned. We have found ourselves on the outside looking in, wondering if things could be better or ever really change. We all long for a more loving father, a brother or sister who will lay down their life for us, a place in a family where we can safely be ourselves.

When we live out our new identity as a family — God's family — we offer that very thing to a waiting and watching world. The truth is, we do have a perfectly loving Father. Our Brother Jesus has laid his life down for us, and we no longer need to hide in shame for the things we have done or that have been done to us.

We were created to live in grace-based relationships, which is why true gospel communities are an irresistible call to return home. That family represents the open arms of God and a place at his dinner table.

At this point, the missional community decided that they *had* to throw Kirstan a party, but that's a story that I'll save for chapter 11, when we look at how celebrations are a normal rhythm of life that offer great opportunities to display the gospel. You're gonna love it!

FAMILY PORTRAIT

If you compared your picture of a healthy family to your average experience of church, would the two be significantly different? What does a healthy, loving family look like? How does it "feel," and what are the basic functions and relational bonds? How often do the members see each other, hang out, eat, work, and play together?

Let's compare this to most of our experiences of church. Does the church function more like a weekly meeting, business, or institution? What is your motivation for "going to church"? Is it to support one another and display what God is like to a waiting world, or is it to "check the box" and meet some spiritual obligation or cultural expectation?

Ultimately, it is not the things we *do* that make us a family, but rather the stuff we care about, display, and participate in because we *get to* — because of who we are together. We know this to be the case, because many of us have seen or been a part of families that *do* a lot of things together and yet have little love, genuine affection, or concern for one another. The things we choose to do out of love and deference to one another are what bind us together and create a family.

BORN NEEDY

When you were a baby, your parents and perhaps siblings, aunts, uncles, or grandparents were there to feed, clothe, and wipe you and to care for your every need. God created us needy so we would require others and *want* him.

In the New Testament, the church family is compared to a body, with everyone being a different needy and helpful part.

> The body is not made up of one part but of many.... The eye cannot say to the hand, "I don't need you!" And the head cannot say to the feet, "I don't need you!" On the contrary, those parts of the body that seem to be weaker are indispensable.... God has put the body together ... so that there should be no division in the body, but that its parts should have equal concern for each other. If one part suffers, every part suffers with it; if one part is honored, every part rejoices with it.[3]

FAMILY

A family knows one another (all the parts) and should know if anyone is hurting or in need or when it's time to celebrate! Let me quickly take you through some of the ways our community lives together because of our family identity.

FAMILY DINNER NIGHT

As if it is carved into sacred stone, our missional community gets together for a weekly family dinner night. These collaborative meals are usually simple, sometimes elaborate, often thrown together, but always warm and full of acceptance. It is a needed bright spot in our week and a time when anyone and everyone is invited in. At times we will take Communion together and go around speaking good news to each other, pushing back the hurts and disappointments of the week and reminding one another of what is now true of us because of Jesus. Afterward everyone helps clean up, making sure there is no leftover mess.

As a family, we practice an "open door policy" with one another. I know that I can stop by the homes or apartments of those in my community at any time and it will be no big deal. It works in reverse too; my friends know that they can stop by our house anytime (I've noticed that the single guys seem to practice this more around dinnertime).

This may freak you out a little. You may be thinking, *Whoa, how do you have any time to yourself? What about boundaries?* There have been times when my wife, Tina, and I have been sitting on the couch in the evening having a glass of wine together and the doorbell has rung. "Hey, Caesar. Hi, Tina. What are you guys doing tonight?" And I will say, "Hey, Nick, how you doing, brother? Tina and I were just sitting here watching this romantic comedy together, and I, um, was kind of hoping for a happy ending . . . if you know what I mean. [*Wink*] So unless there is some emergency or you really need us right now, let's get together tomorrow if that's cool."

Because of the openness and trust we have with one another, we not only have the freedom to open our homes, but we also have the freedom to say, "Thanks for stopping by, but now is not a great time." We all know this and respect this reality.

One surprising winter day, we actually had a snowstorm in Tacoma, a pretty rare occurrence. Here, even after just a few flakes start to fall, everything, including schools and businesses, shuts down. On this occasion, we actually got a few inches of snow on the ground (a catastrophe to some), and as I watched the snow falling from my living room picture window, most of the folks from our missional community came trudging up the street, throwing pathetically small snowballs at one another and at my face in the window. Since they didn't have work or classes, they made their way to our house for breakfast and a movie.

That's what a family does!

One afternoon when I was having a meeting at my house with a few leaders from our community, Jeff walked into my house and went straight to the kitchen. He opened up my refrigerator. "I am starving," he said. "What do we have for lunch in here?"

The others who were there meeting with us were a little surprised. No knocking, no asking — he was just being a brother. Why was this so shocking? Jeff and I live just a few doors apart from each other and have always treated each other's homes, tools, cars, and food like they were "family property." He is my brother (because of the gospel), and I love that he treats me and our things this way and that I get to do the same. It serves as a constant reminder that everything we have is really God's and has been given to us to use and share for his purposes.

When we first moved to Tacoma to start Soma and learn to live like a family on mission, I needed to add a couple of bedrooms and a new bath to our third-floor attic space. My daughters insisted that this little haven upstairs be theirs, so our entire community helped with the demolition of old, dirty flooring and removal of decades of junk that had accumulated in our hundred-year-old home. Those with actual carpentry and plumbing skills helped get that part of the job done, and those who could paint and clean did that. It became a community project, filling this new living space with life and laughter long before moving my daughters into their new rooms. Every doorknob, lighting fixture, and unplanned paint drip remind me of this diverse and beautiful family God has given us.

We play together, go away on vacations or retreats together, and we party — often. There is always something to celebrate and be thankful for in this group: a new job, the birth of a child, a clean bill of health from a doctor, or something as simple as a good grade for a completed course in college. I can honestly say that I have never had more fun than with my friends in this community on mission. We have a certain freedom to laugh, joke, and tease when we are increasingly free to be who God says we are *together*.

We've had great experiences together cheering on someone's child at a soccer game or a single mom's daughter at her dance recital. And my favorite celebrations are when we gather at the beach to hear testimonies of new life and identity found in Christ, baptizing new brothers and sisters into this family.

Of course, we also cry together and at times argue with one another. When my close friend Jayne's father passed away, we all felt a great loss with and for her. We learned that the best thing we could do for Jayne in that time was just be with her — no great words of wisdom, just the gentle comfort of presence and shared tears. I have also argued with this beautiful, smart sister who has a personality so very similar to mine in many ways. We have deeply hurt each other, as often happens with family, and have needed to seek forgiveness from each other. These times are hard, but they always produce a rich fruit that only comes from believing the best of one another and siding with God on behalf of one another. When the family sees arguments that end with seeking and granting forgiveness, they witness the truth of the gospel at work.

BUT SOMETIMES IT'S HARD ...

Any of the above examples and stories could spin off in a bad direction if we didn't live with a gospel focus and intentionality. If my life is all about my comfort and feeding my preferences, then all of that stuff would be frightening and impossible to sustain. But in light of the love we have been shown, it is a pleasure to live in ways that show what the Father is like.

After living in community for a while, we had to find a new balance and die to some old, self-centered patterns and rhythms. With a table full of family and friends most nights, our daughters started wondering when we were going to get some time alone, just them with their mom and dad, "like we used to." They wanted a weekly dinner night to be one of those times. We agreed with them and asked our community to take a break from hanging around on Wednesday nights for dinner. We let them know that they could come over before or after dinner but that we were going to have a little time as a family with just our daughters. But after a couple of months of these dinners alone, our daughters began to ask if it was okay if they invited "just this one friend," and then another, over to join us.

"My friend Melissa really needs some time with us because she has some questions I think you could answer for her, Dad." And soon after, "Would it be okay if we had Terry over, just this week? His parents are going through a divorce, and he needs a family right now."

Over time we learned that we could carve out those special family times as needed without feeling the need to mandate a rigid, unbreakable schedule. We needed to allow space for God to break into our rhythms and continue to use Team K (the name we use to refer to our family) whenever he needed to.

This life lived as a family on mission is always under attack from our great enemy, Satan, because he doesn't want us to live this way, showing others what God is truly like.

Regularly someone will be misunderstood or take the words, actions, or attitudes of another in the wrong way. People have left our community over misconceptions and twisted words that never got dealt with. We need a gentle yet consistent commitment to keep short accounts with one another and clean up messes and perceived offenses as soon as we are aware of them. Our words can be like bullets in a gun that need to be holstered or aimed in the right direction.

TAKE COVER!

Unlike Ralphie and his relatively harmless Red Ryder BB gun from *A Christmas Story*, sometimes things can get a little more serious — and dangerous — in a family. Tina and I had been in Eastern Europe for a few weeks working with church planters, and it was a good trip, but we were anxious to get back home to our family and friends. Some of them were staying at our house, keeping an eye on things while we were away. Right.

A few hours after getting home and unpacking, I plopped down to watch a little TV and catch up with folks on what had been going on in our community. Hugging one of the couch pillows to my chest and relaxing back onto the couch, I noticed the pillow had a seven- or eight-inch rip in it that had obviously been repaired by a professional. I asked my son, who was in town visiting while we were gone, "What happened to this pillow?"

"I'm afraid to tell you; you'll be angry."

"I'm already a little angry; just tell me what happened," I replied.

"Did you notice the couch?"

I looked down at the place where the pillow had been nestled and noticed another long, already-sewn tear in the cushion.

"What the heck happened here?"

To make a long, horrifying story short, while we were away in Europe, a young man from our community was admiring my son's .45 caliber military service pistol. He had managed to turn off the safeties and shoot the gun through our pillow and cushion, lodging a hollow-point bullet into the frame of our couch. All of this happened with a house full of people present!

Yep, he was right. I was a little angry.

"Was anyone hurt?" I asked. Thank God, nobody was. I shivered at the thought that someone could have been severely hurt or killed. We could have ended up with a bullet hole in my TV or out the side of the house. All in all, the outcome wasn't bad considering what might have happened. It is times like this that I'm reminded that people are infinitely more valuable than my furniture or any of the other things I tend to worry about getting "messed up" or broken.

Some people might never want to let anyone use their home after an incident like that. But I am reminded of how many times God has entrusted his "stuff" and people into my hands and I have messed it up or acted irresponsibly. Yet he keeps trusting me and walking forward in relationship with me — a total knucklehead.

I want to be more like that. Bullet holes and all.

WHO'S YOUR DADDY?

Imagine that you've been living in your house for a few years, going about your busy life: working, raising a family, going to school — all the normal stuff of life that keeps us focused on — well, ourselves. What would you do if all of a sudden you realized your own father, sister, or brother was alone — in terrible need — and had been living right next door?

Maybe they are, and you never noticed.

Who does the Bible say is in "our family"? Is it just Christians, or in a sense, is it really everyone? I guess the answer to the question of who you will treat like family is best answered by asking, would you treat Jesus like a member of your own family? Jesus told his disciples a parable one day to help them grasp the reality of how he sees everyone and how he hopes his followers will see and treat others.

> " 'I was hungry and you gave me something to eat, I was thirsty and you gave me something to drink, I was a stranger and you invited me in, I needed clothes and you clothed me, I was sick and you looked after me, I was in prison and you came to visit me. . . . Truly I tell you, whatever you did for one of the least of these *brothers* and *sisters* of mine, you did for me.' " [4]

I see it like this: We have some brothers and sisters out there who are estranged from Dad. They don't trust him and stopped coming to holiday meals and family functions long ago. They are having a hard time believing that Dad really loves them. But he does, enough that he sent his Son, our own Brother, to rescue and save them. It cost him his life, but that's how much Dad and his Son love them and want them restored to a full and wonderful life in this family.

So let's stop worrying about who's in or who's out, saved or unsaved. Let's treat everyone like family — the way God does. God is in the adoption business. He wants you and everyone else in his family. He says, *I've got some pretty weird kids — but you'll grow to love them.*

THINGS TO THINK ABOUT

Have you traditionally seen your faith or Christianity as something private and a solo adventure?

What shifts in your heart as you begin to believe that God has given you a family — his family — to walk through all of life with?

How do you normally respond to those in your church who are different than you or who are harder to be around? Why might God have placed them in your life?

How could your "Christian life" begin to look more like "family life"?

Chapter 4

MISSIONARIES

*We are sent by God to restore all
people and things to himself.*

IT FELT LIKE we were on one of those extreme travel shows.
After several flights with extended layovers and rapid-fire questions from uniformed guards in long security lines, we boarded an
old, sketchy Russian helicopter that took us over the muddy bay
to where we landed in Freetown. After nearly twenty-four hours of
exhausting travel, we had finally arrived at our destination in the
capital of war-torn Sierra Leone.

That was just the beginning of the full-out assault on our senses.
For the next two weeks, we experienced heat and humidity that
made us feel like we were living in a sauna. We ate local foods that
tasted like two-week-old leftovers that would normally be thrown
away back home. The poverty of the local people was crushing as
the smell of death and violence still hung thick in the air. You could
see in the eyes of the people that they were losing hope.

We had traveled all this way and gone deep into the jungle to
help deliver housing materials and aid to villages that had been
ravaged by rebel soldiers. The people in these villages, mostly
Muslims, were grateful. Their constant handshakes and offers

from the elders to sit and have tea with us were humbling. But the thing they were most appreciative of and impressed by was that we were actually there. To *be with* them. Being present with them in their darkest hour made all the difference in the world.

If you have ever been on a short-term missions trip, you may know what this is like. You experience so many challenges, fears, and victories that your heart comes alive in a new way. You are submitted to and partnering with God like never before. Your exhausting days, nights, and prayers are so filled with kingdom purpose and intention that you feel like you could stay and live like this forever.

But then you fly home. Back to "normal" life.

Responsibilities and routines, even Sunday church attendance, kick back in, and soon the memories of your amazing adventure with Jesus over in Africa fade and are reduced to a few favorite stories and photographs. Why couldn't we just live like that — like missionaries — *here*? Every day?

I have spent years traveling around the world "doing" missions, and each time, upon returning home, my heart has ached. While in those other nations, with the Christians living there, our lives together looked and felt very much like what I read in the New Testament book of Acts. The believers in both cases lived their lives completely oriented and prioritized around Jesus' kingdom, and were filled and phenomenally empowered by the Holy Spirit for great adventures.

I want that. Today. In my neighborhood!

THE FAMILY BUSINESS

Our God is a missionary God, and we see his missionary heart displayed right in the beginning of the biblical story, in Genesis 3. After Adam and Eve had chosen to rebel against God and had eaten from the Tree of the Knowledge of Good and Evil, they hid themselves among the trees. And what did God do? He went looking for them, calling out, "Where are you? Where are you?" Immediately after God's beloved image bearers chose a life of self-rule — one in which they thought they could manage the knowledge of good and evil, right and wrong, for themselves — God went on a rescue mission. He went looking for them. That is his heart.

Later in the story, when God's special people, the Israelites, had sinned and rejected him, he instructed them to build a great tent called a tabernacle. He told Moses, "Build me a place were I can dwell among the people whom I love!" It was as if God were saying, *I just have to get closer to my people; I want to live among them to guide and protect them.*

Then God sent his own Son on the ultimate missionary trip, to this earth, to rescue and restore all of humanity. He came to be one of us, to live among us — to *be with* us.

Then Jesus did and said something that changed the world and our lives forever. "Jesus said, 'Peace be with you! As the Father has sent me, I am sending you.' And with that he breathed on them and said, 'Receive the Holy Spirit' "[1]

Amazingly, when Jesus left to go and be with his Father in heaven, he sent his own Spirit to live *inside* us. Even closer than walking around and hanging out with us, God now lives *inside* his people, within his family!

And just as Jesus' Father sent him, the Father now sends us. The word *missionary* literally means "sent one." If you are a Christian, you are a "sent one," a missionary. As I said earlier, this is our new, true identity.

NATURAL-BORN MISSIONARIES

Remember when I said that the biggest blessing to the folks in Sierra Leone was that we were there with them? That incarnational aspect is the most important thing about being a missionary.

The word *incarnation* comes from a Latin word that means "flesh."

To incarnate is to put flesh on something or someone. Jesus came in the flesh (incarnate) and wore the scratchy robes and sandals of the people he lived among. He grew his hair and beard. He ate what the people ate and experienced everything they experienced, temptations and all!

Here is a hypothetical question I am almost certain you could answer: If you and your family, maybe with a few close friends, were called, sent, and fully funded to go to another country and establish the gospel — to start a church and see people come to faith in Jesus — what would you immediately begin to do? What would your life consist of? How would you *be* with the people there?

I have asked many people this question, and their answers are always remarkably similar. "We would start by getting to know the language of the local people. We would eat what and where they eat, start to dress more like them, and adopt some of their customs. We would shop at the same places over and over to get to know the shop and restaurant owners. We would look for ways to be a blessing to them, serving them in simple ways as a display of God's love for them. We would need to live as much like them as possible and build relationships over time."

That would be a pretty good start, don't you think?

ONE OF THEM

When we first moved to Tacoma to start living like *real* missionaries, we pretty much started with these same basic ideas.

The clothing my wife, daughters, and I wore began to change. In the Pacific Northwest, people tend to dress in flannel shirts, ala the grunge music era that has never ended; they grow their hair into dreadlocks; they wear those heavy leather Doc Martens boots; and they have goatees. We were definitely "incarnating."

MISSIONARIES

We started to eat out locally — *a lot*. Our favorite restaurant became this little breakfast place called Shakabrah. The name is a Hawaiian word meaning, "Hang loose, bro!" That pretty much sums up this place. The breakfasts are enormous, and the clientele includes people from every imaginable walk of life. We ended up buying this place, but more on that later.

We found a couple local pubs and learned to drink bitter, hoppy microbrews. Since the regional politics are very different than where I was raised, I had to decide whether I loved my political views and party affiliation more than the people Jesus sent us to be with. Would I let my opinions, or those of others, become barriers to real relationship?

Over time everything began to change as we started to radically reprioritize our lives around the people God had sent us to.

Let's just say we have a few more tattoos these days than we used to.

But, hey, you might be thinking, *I thought the Bible says we are to be in the world but not of it. What's that mean?*

One of Jesus' close friends, John, recorded him praying, "My prayer is not that you take them out of the world but that you protect them from the evil one" [2] All of this is a heart issue. Who is your dressing, eating, and drinking — or not — focused on? For whose glory are you doing these things and living this way? Jesus rebuked the Pharisees in Matthew 23, saying, "Woe to you, teachers of the law and Pharisees, you hypocrites! You clean the outside of the cup and dish, but inside they are full of greed and self-indulgence. Blind Pharisee! First clean the inside of the cup and dish, and then the outside also will be clean" [3]

The heart behind all of our incarnation must be love. It must be to show Jesus to others, to live as he did so they will know his Father. It is not some external adherence to the culture around us that makes us missionaries; it is having the heart of Jesus who is both *with* and *for* the people.[4]

The church was never meant to be a building out on the edge of town. Jesus intended us to be a people of love and service who live out and proclaim the good news of his kingdom. God's family should be woven into the very fabric of the culture, shouldering sin and pain in the lives of others. If we were to go away or cease to exist in the community, people should cry out, "No! They can't go away; they've loved us so well!"

HARVESTTIME

My buddy Chuck, who lives like a missionary in Jonesboro, Arkansas, is definitely what we northerners refer to as a "good ol' boy." He's been a lawyer for years and is often referred to as "the mayor" because he seems to know everyone in town and is always — *always* — helping somebody. I just love hanging out with Chuck and letting his gentle spirit and positive outlook rub off on me.

A few years ago, Chuck and his family came up with a pretty creative way to get into the rhythm of their neighborhood around Halloween time. Even though many Christians sort of put a ban on this holiday, they saw it as an opportunity to be good missionaries. They went around handing out flyers announcing a "Treats in the Street Halloween Parade" they were organizing for the kids and parents who lived around them.

They went to ninety-four homes and personally invited everyone to set up decorated tables at the end of their driveways and hand out candy as the kids (of all ages) paraded by in costume. They hoped to help provide a fun and safe trick-or-treat experience for the kids and an easy opportunity to get to know one another.

Everyone met at Chuck and Lindy's place at 5:15 after work and marched around the neighborhood, up one block and down the other, then back to Chuck's place where he had a big fire pit blazing in the backyard. They had more than a hundred people parade around, including forty to fifty kids! They had a bounce house for the kids and huge, steaming pots of chili for everyone to enjoy. The parade was a big success and has become an annual event.

Celebrating like this can easily lead to something much greater than just handing out candy and sharing a bowl of chili together. Chuck and his missional community all truly believe they are a family, and they desire to live out that reality while inviting others to join them.

After the parade, out back of the house, Chuck set down his bowl of chili and very casually said to everyone, "We want to get to know our neighbors. We're Christians, and God says to love your neighbors, and we have not been loving you. We don't even know most of you! Can we talk about needs that anyone might have here in the neighborhood?"

A few people expressed needs at school that they knew about, the desire to keep an eye on one another's homes at night, and a couple of other things like that. Nothing too startling or "heavy" — pretty normal stuff — with the entire exchange lasting only three or four minutes. A little while after this sharing time, an elderly woman rolled up in her wheelchair and asked, "Are you serious about wanting to help meet needs around here?"

"Yes, ma'am, we are!" Chuck replied.

This sixty-eight-year-old disabled woman named Lois shared privately that there were four generations of family living in her house and a homeless friend in the basement. She told Chuck and a few others that her house was in bad need of repair. There was a hole in the roof where the rain poured in, many other things were broken, and she did not have the strength or money to fix these things.

The community went to work immediately that week. They started cutting, raking, and trimming the yard that Lois's ten dogs had completely destroyed. Then they got to work on fixing the leaky roof. When they moved inside, what they encountered was truly a shock to their senses. The smell was like a punch in the face — so bad that some of the women who had come to help clean had to leave until the fifty-plus bags of garbage were removed.

As the work and weeks went by, Lois and her family began to come over for dinner with Chuck and Lindy. They were truly becoming part of the family. Over time they joined in the rhythms of Chuck's missional community and started taking part in everything they did, including going with them to Sunday church services.

Later that year, Chuck had the privilege of baptizing Lois, her homeless friend who still lives in the house, and one of her granddaughters — right there in Chuck's backyard in plain sight of all the neighbors! They had come to believe that God was their Father and that he had sent his other kids to love them and show what life in his family is really like. They trusted Jesus for their salvation and came to trust this family as their own.

Lois has become a peacemaker and a missionary in this healing environment. God is transforming her identity as she is starting to believe what he says about her is true — that all of her messy past does not define her. She has a new identity. Chuck says that Lois and her family have taught them more about how to love people than a million Bible studies ever could have.

I wonder what kind of Halloween costume Lois will be wearing next fall as she wheels herself around the neighborhood with all of the kids?

HOMEGROWN OR INGROWN?

As our group of friends grew and multiplied in Tacoma, it became really easy just to spend time being together, to focus on those of us within our community of believers. So we started praying for greater intentionality to go — to *be with* — to incarnate among those around us, to live as the missionaries we had become. And God showed us that there were opportunities all around us.

Here are a few examples of what I like to call "low-hanging fruit," those situations that present themselves as easy step-on points to relationship and mission.

My neighborhood has a very high concentration of single parents with kids. Our missional community at the time also had a couple of single moms who brought great insight and ideas on how we could serve the needs of their peers. God led us to love and incarnate among these young mothers as we discipled some of them to faith. Along the way we paid bills, moved furniture, tutored, taxied, babysat, partied, laughed, cried, and sometimes even fought with these modern-day "widows and orphans."

For several years our community helped host a "Back to School Night" in the neighborhood. We handed out hundreds of backpacks full of school supplies. We set up haircutting stations and had local stylists come and give free haircuts to the kids who wanted a new 'do before school started the next day. A local clinic that partnered with us provided checkups and immunizations. And we handed out mountains of grilled burgers, hot dogs, chips, and soda. The line for this event ran down the block. We met even more of the moms and their children around us through serving them this way each year.

Most of the things we've learned to do as missionaries just involve normal, everyday activities but are infused with gospel intentionality. For example, my longtime friend Todd loves to smoke a pipe, especially sitting out back in his yard in the cool, crisp, evening air. He started having very impromptu "pipe nights" with guys in his missional community, men from work, and others from around the neighborhood. I have attended some of these smoke fests, and I always leave amazed at the conversation we get into with one another: marriage, faith, parenting, work, sports — it all comes up.

Naturally, our faith seeps into each conversation. Good news has a way of doing that. These are not forced evangelistic times, but these easy, casual pipe nights have led to more than a few people coming to faith in Jesus.

Some of these same guys' wives started inviting other moms from the neighborhood to join them when they would take their kids to the park to burn off steam. No big deal; they were going anyway — only now they had a greater reason to go! That naturally led to trading babysitting favors and such as their relationships deepened.

Are you catching the normalcy of all of this?

Friends of mine in Los Angeles started doing happy hour after work once or twice a week. They wanted to open their homes in ways that the culture — their friends — already loved and enjoyed. A quick drink and a snack with friends and neighbors quickly became a local favorite.

Here in Tacoma, we have a very talented group of musicians and songwriters in our community. Several of them saw an opportunity to live as missionaries among the other singer-songwriters in our city. They started hosting simple food and song "circles," and over time this group of artists became a tight-knit family, writing and recording dozens of songs together and hosting a songwriters' showcase at a local café or club each month. The songs they write and perform express a new or growing faith in Jesus and how their lives are changing in light of God's story.

I could tell literally hundreds of these stories if I had enough space, but don't miss this: being a missionary is more about *being* than doing.

BUT SOMETIMES IT'S HARD …

I sometimes find myself thinking, *I don't really want to be here with these people right now.* Or *I would rather just hang out with my*

Christian friends. They understand me better and I feel more comfortable around them. It is often at that time that I'll get a call or text from someone in my community inviting me to go and be a blessing to one of their friends. And I'm reminded that this missionary life isn't a lone-ranger lifestyle. I am a missionary as part of a family.

Even when *I* don't feel like living this out, other brothers and sisters do, and I can go along as support, trusting in the Spirit for new motivation and love outside of my own exhaustible supply. I need this sacred family to repeatedly, lovingly remind me that my missionary Father sent his Son, my Brother, to rescue and save me, giving me his missionary identity. And strength. And wisdom. I need to hear that a lot, because the habits of this life and world seem to squeeze that out of me.

GO AND MAKE

But this lifestyle is not just about hanging out with people and building relationships. If we are not careful, we can end up being the nicest, hippest people in our neighborhoods but still not be leading anyone to walk in the ways of Jesus. It is easy to get distracted and forget about the mission a missionary has: go and make disciples. We must be about helping people grow in their faith and trust in Jesus.

This problem, again, is a heart issue. I have found that it is infinitely easier to be friends with people, maybe even serve them in sacrificial ways, than to intentionally disciple them — apprentice them — in their faith. The reason is fear. I fear they will reject me if I move from doing good things to introducing them to the Good News — Jesus. In those situations, I am actually loving myself more than others, and more than Jesus. I am believing that their faith and walk with God is my responsibility. But God is the One who gives faith, and the Spirit is the One who grants repentance and illuminates the truth.

So the pressure is off!

SKIN DEEP

Countless times after sharing success stories like these, I am asked, "How many hours each week do you expect people to give to this church thing, to living like a missionary?" And I wonder, *Is this a trick question?* All of them! You *are* the church, you *are* a missionary.

I have to be honest with you here. After living this way for nearly a decade now, I don't think there is a huge difference between being a missionary here in America compared with living this way in a foreign country. People are people, and we all have many of the same needs and fears.

The biggest difference here is that I constantly feel two things pulling at me: my past experience of "going to church" instead of being the church, and my lack of faith that the gospel is truly good news for everyone and everything. My tendency is to revert back to making everything an event or weekly meeting or teaching time, thinking that if people just heard one more good sermon or did one more Bible study, they would really "get it." If that were the case, then why didn't Jesus just broadcast some good news really loudly from heaven so that everyone on the planet could hear? It's because the Good News — the gospel — is not a set of facts. The Good News is a person.

Jesus came to show the world what God his Father is truly like. He came as a missionary. That's why we "go." That's why we must be out there too, among people, with flesh on so that they too might experience the love of God.

JOHNNY RED AND A DIZZLE

My mom and dad were great people and pretty much your average Christians who "attended church" a couple of times each week for more than thirty years. They gave at least 10 percent of their income to the church and more to missionaries around the world.

MISSIONARIES

When Tina, the kids, and I first moved out to Tacoma, my parents had a hard time grasping just what it was we were trying to do or be as these "missionaries." Previously, when I was a pastor at a very large suburban church near Chicago, they understood my life of meetings at the church building every day. They loved to come watch me preach in front of thousands of people on Sunday with my face twelve feet tall on the jumbo video screens. "But what *exactly* do you do *now*?" they asked. So they decided to come for a visit to see and experience this missional lifestyle for themselves.

They arrived the day before we threw a very large Labor Day party and cookout for a real eclectic mix. A bunch of "regular" folks who were my neighbors came. Some kids came with their parents. Several guys and gals came from my missional community, which at the time was composed of mostly twentysomething hipsters, many of whom played in rock bands. They brought some of their friends and girlfriends along. And then there were my parents.

Kind of a freak show really.

But my dad dove in and started making the rounds at the party, talking with everyone! He ended up in a conversation with a good friend of mine we called Dizzle. ("What is a *dizzle*?" he later asked me.) Dad encouraged him in his new teaching job that was going poorly and told him he would pray for him. Weeks later Diz told me that everything had turned around for him at work and to be sure to thank my dad for praying for him!

Dad also spent a lot of time that day talking to a young, long-haired, supertattooed rocker who went by the name of Johnny Red. Johnny was a drug addict and was using several drugs at the time. My father recounted for Johnny his own struggle with alcoholism and how Jesus had taken that addiction and destructive lifestyle from him, saving his life and marriage. He encouraged Johnny not to try harder but to trust Jesus more. I could hardly believe what I was seeing and hearing. Dad was tearing up this missionary thing!

Later that week, our community went on a walk around my neighborhood. I asked them to notice, as we walked around, anyone or anything that was broken, messed up, or not the way God desired them or it to be. Both my mom, with her "bad leg," and my dad insisted on coming along. We stopped in the middle of our outing to discuss what we observed.

There were run-down houses, broken fences in need of repair, and a park full of trash. We overheard a young couple having a very heated discussion. The husband was not very happy about something and seemed to be drunk. We prayed and asked God to show us which of these people or things he would have us to be a part of restoring and healing in the weeks ahead. Then we walked home. There were no crazy epiphanies, but we were listening.

Afterward, my dad said to me, "I have never done anything like that before, but I think I'm getting it. Most people in your city would never go to church to hear about Jesus, so you are taking the church and Jesus to them. Is that right?"

Yes, Dad. I couldn't have put it better myself.

THINGS TO THINK ABOUT

What would change in your life if you lived like a full-time missionary — right where you are?

Where, what, or who is your personal "mission field"?

Could it be said that you are a friend of sinners? Do you have close relationships of trust with several not-yet believers? If not very many, why?

What types of activities could you begin to engage in as a missionary to build more relationships with others who do not yet walk with Jesus?

Chapter 5

SERVANTS

*We are servants like Jesus who serve
others as a way of life.*

SOMETIMES STORMS COME IN WAVES. Wanda originally
moved to Tacoma after Hurricane Katrina had taken everything
she owned, leaving her penniless, homeless, and hopeless. She
came as part of a relocation service the government offered, but
after months of being unable to secure regular work, she was now
being evicted from her apartment that very day. And her seven-
teen-year-old daughter, several months pregnant at the time, and
her diabetic, aging mother were also being put out on the curb.

After making some calls, we found out that Wanda did not have
the credit needed to qualify for an apartment, much less one with
three bedrooms that would meet her needs. So we called in a
few favors and were able to find her an apartment that day. But
it required that she come up with a security deposit and three
months' rent before the landlord would accept her. Unfortunately,
she had none of the money she needed.

So our community scraped together the required deposit and
advance rent. We called everyone who was not at work that day,
secured a box truck, and moved Wanda's possessions over to
the new place. She and the family were, as you can imagine, very

thankful. They had woken up that day expecting to be out in the street, and God had sent his family to serve her, showing his love in tangible ways.

We asked her if she desired help to break the cycle of poverty and debt she lived in. "Oh yes, for sure!" she said. "Y'all are amazing!" We helped her set up a budget that week, showed her ways to save money on food and other expenses, and made sure her daughter was getting the medical attention she needed.

This was definitely the gospel with skin on.

THE GOOD NEWS IN LIVING COLOR

As a kid, I loved watching the movie *The Wizard of Oz*. It was televised once a year, and like clockwork my family would line up, eyes glazed in wonder, tearing through bags of my dad's favorite potato chips and bottles of twenty-five-cent "local pop" in front of our twenty-five-inch RCA TV. My favorite part (other than when the wicked witch finally gets water thrown on her and melts to nothing under her big black hat) was when the movie went from black and white to luscious, dripping color! I would wait for that part when everything seemed to explode with life.

For a lot of people, Christianity and going to church, or even reading the Bible, is stuck in "black and white," mere words on a page. It's when we live out our identity as servants, making the kingdom of God real and tangible, that we help people *experience* the good news of the gospel in full, living color. And this is not just some evangelistic tactic; this is true for us too. We all need frequent living examples of how extraordinarily and sacrificially we have been served by Jesus.

COSMIC DEMOTION OR ETERNAL UPGRADE?

Fully God and fully human, Jesus took on the role of a servant. He gave his life, even to the point of death, so that others could experience salvation, peace, and restoration. He said, "The Son of Man did not come to be served, but to serve, and to give his life as a ransom for many."[1] Have you ever thought about how far King Jesus stooped in order to take on the form of a human?

To so humble himself and put on the skin, clothing, relational shift, and sore muscles required to walk among us as a servant is hard to grasp, not to mention how much cooler heaven must be compared with here on earth! The president of the United States coming to your neighborhood and picking up trash for three years with no pay, and at times great opposition, would not come close to the posture of humility our great Servant-King Jesus took on.

IT'S HARD TO IMPRESS ANGELS

Jesus, creator of the universe, the one who spoke worlds into existence, was eternally living in perfect relational harmony with his Father and the Spirit. Then the day arrived. Angels had been waiting for ages for this event. "He's going down there; he's really going to do it. Look, today's the day!"

There were no parades, no fanfare. He arrived as a baby, born to a teenage virgin, and spent his first days as a human wrapped in rags and lying in a dirty feed trough that the animals still looked to for dinner. (Maybe that's why they are always hanging around baby Jesus in all of those nativity scenes.) He grows up pretty much like every other Jewish boy in his neighborhood: not broke — his dad has skills — but there's never much extra. He has no special abilities or talents to speak of and doesn't really stand out. He's a good boy, does as his parents say, and grows into an average young man from Nazareth.

Then, after he is filled with God's own Spirit, everything changes. He becomes a healer, teacher, and servant like no one has ever seen before. He spends the next three years of his life caring for people, mending their broken bones, hearts, and misconceptions about his Father. He lives completely focused on the needs of others for his Father's glory.

He takes upon himself *all* of the broken hearts, attitudes, and delusions of self-rule that have separated the people he loves from his Father. Then, in the most brilliant display of his servant identity, he dies.

But that's not the end of the story.

Victory breaks back into this world as the Spirit of God brings this humble Servant back to life — *forever* — his life the clarifying pinnacle of what God's story is all about. Then he invites others to go and live their lives in the same way, also filled by his Spirit.

Those who accept his offer of new life now live forever, for the sake of others, as part of what we call the church.

W3 LIFESTYLE

Jesus wanted his disciples (and us) to remember this relational dynamic: "No servant is greater than his master, nor is a messenger greater than the one who sent him."[2] In fact, a couple of chapters later Jesus repeats these words to his disciples.[3] Apparently he felt they needed to be reminded. I wonder what was going on in their lives to prompt him to repeat himself. I wonder what was going on in their hearts.

I wonder what is going on in *your* heart right now as you contemplate all of this?

As the noteworthy British pastor George Müller said, "It ill becomes the servant to seek to be rich, and great, and honored in this world where his Lord was poor, and mean, and despised."

In trying to cultivate the heart to consistently serve others in our community, we are trying to adopt what we call a "W3 lifestyle":

serving anyone God brings into our lives with *whatever* needs doing, *whenever* it is needed, and *wherever* it leads us.

On the surface, that lifestyle might seem overwhelming, but living as a family of servants is awesome because it means that when I see a need or one arises, I know that I am not always (or even usually) called to meet that need alone. In fact, sometimes I see something that needs addressing, and I call someone else in the family and ask them to handle it.

Just so we're clear, Jesus did not *have* to come, serve us, and lay down his life. He *chose* to. Out of love for his Father and a desire to restore us to a right and loving relationship with him, Jesus paid the price for our sin that we never could. He served us in a way that he alone could. Even while we still held our defiant fists in the air, claiming self-rule and building our own kingdoms, Jesus heard our cries, saw our need, and did something about it. He shoulders our sin; he cleans up our messes.

Again, our attitude should not be that we have to or *should* serve others; rather, we should be excited that we *get to* serve others as a display of the great gospel, in light of how utterly and sacrificially Jesus has served us! We show the world what he is like as we live out our identity as servants.

ALL DRESSED UP AND SOMEWHERE TO GO

A few times each year, our larger church family of Soma here in Tacoma hosts guests from around the world for a weeklong immersion experience with us in community. We call this week Soma School. Participants spend the week living with one of our missional communities, in their homes, learning many of these same core thoughts about our new identity in Christ and helping to serve those in need around us. It is a pretty high-octane week of discipleship and a life-changing experience for most.

One summer I invited a few young men who were here with us for

Soma School to help me serve my elderly neighbor Hal. He was attempting to do some pretty intense landscaping projects and was getting nowhere fast. In just a couple of hours, these young bucks and I were able to complete the job that would have taken him several days to accomplish. Hal was extremely thankful and a little surprised that these friends of mine would jump in and work so hard. He invited us into his home to have refreshments with him. We accepted and headed in for what we imagined would be a soda or glass of cold lemonade in his kitchen.

Hal proceeded to take us downstairs to his basement where he had built for himself a complete pub! I'm not talking about some little raised countertop and a few stools. No, sir. Hal had a fully stocked bar with beer taps, neon signs, electronic games, swivel chairs — the whole deal. It felt like we had been transported back in time, and maybe to Bavaria or someplace like that. His wife, Gail, jumped to the task and began to pour us whatever drinks we wanted. These young guys' jaws dropped open. Hal's creativity and ingenuity to build this old-school pub into his basement was impressive to say the least.

In the course of our conversation, I casually invited Hal to our Memorial Day cookout we were planning for a few days later. "Maybe I'll come and wear my old uniform," he said. "I was in World War II, you know."

"You should really do that, Hal," I said. "That would be so cool!"

Well, guess what? A couple of days later, on Memorial Day, here comes Hal, slowly walking down our block, dressed fully and proudly in his snappy World War II uniform and medals, his oxygen bottle swinging at his hip with the clear tubing running up to his nostrils, and a bowl of potato salad in his hand. He looked great. No, he looked downright remarkable!

Later at the cookout, out on my deck in the backyard, I looked over the diversity of friends, family, and neighbors that had assembled to celebrate and be together: my wife and daughters, my son and a couple of his Marine Corp buddies, a few of my new, young, tattooed and pierced friends, and a dozen or so of my neighbors, including Hal in uniform along with his wife, Gail. I asked for everyone's attention. Looking around at everyone and then up at the bright blue sky, I said, "I am superthankful for today and for all of you. Would it be okay if I took a moment to thank God too?"

Turning to Hal, I said, "First I want to say a big thanks to Hal today. Hal, thanks for laying down your life and preferences to serve this nation all those years ago and to help provide the freedom we now enjoy. When you did that you were such a picture of what Jesus is like. Thanks for that!" Then I prayed, "Father, I am so thankful for this beautiful, sunny day and for all of our friends and my family. We get to party when we want to and enjoy each other in peace and freedom. Thanks for Hal, and thank you, too, for the amazing food we have today! Amen." My prayer was short, sweet, and to the point — and no churchy language or holding hands.

Well, you would have thought that Hal was going to explode with pride for the honor we had just showed him. Our connection and trust went to a new level that day, and our conversations changed and went deeper after that. In leading those young men to be servants — part of their discipleship — it also allowed us to serve and honor Hal in a way that changed our relationship forever. I was also given the chance to model prayer and thankfulness that pointed to Jesus and our heavenly Father and was entirely appropriate for the situation without creeping out my non-Christian friends.

IMAGE BEARERS

I love pointing out how someone is an example of the Good News or how something they did reminds me of Jesus. It is a powerful experience for them and a humble and surprising form of "evangelism" as you connect their life directly to God's plans and purposes.

You have never looked into the face of another person that is not an image bearer of God. No matter what they have done in their life — no matter how filthy, sinful, addicted, violent, or confused they may seem — God's image is never completely marred or removed from them.

Or from you, for that matter. Jesus said that any good act of service we do for one another is really done for him.

WITH A LITTLE HELP FROM MY FRIENDS

I had been traveling more than usual, and my gardens and flower beds had become jungle-like. Sadly, I hadn't had the time to get after the yard work in many weeks. But shortly after I arrived home, I was walking out to the garage to take out the trash and noticed that my entire garden had been immaculately weeded! Someone had done a way better job than I do. *Who did this? When did this happen?* I wondered. I asked Tina, but she didn't know.

"It didn't happen when I was here," she said. "Don't look at me."

I never did figure out who blessed me that week, but I sure hope they'll come back again someday soon, because those darn weeds are raising their ugly heads again.

Living life as a family of missionary servants provides endless opportunities to serve one another — not all of them glamorous or fun. As is common in the Pacific Northwest, rain had been pouring down hard for several days in a row in November. The walls and seams in my buddy Greg's basement began dripping water. Then trickling. Then flooding. Making matters much worse, Greg had just finished an elaborate remodel of this space a few months earlier.

Dang.

Someone in our missional community got on the phone and started lining up electric pumps, hoses, and buckets to help stay ahead of the rising flood that threatened to ruin everything down there. For the next forty-eight hours, brothers and sisters in this family took nonstop shifts bailing and pumping water. Greg tried to stay awake for the whole ordeal, but others insisted he get some sleep and go to work the next day. "We've got this for you!" they said.

Fortunately, the rains subsided after another day or two and water stopped flowing in, but the damage had been done. Drywall and carpeting had to be replaced while Greg, Mary, and their kids stayed with friends. In a few weeks, everything was back to normal, the leaks had been permanently patched, and our little family was once again reminded that life in the family of God is a rare privilege.

Over the years of living in community, our folks have spent untold hours babysitting one another's kids for date nights and preparing meals for those who are sick or who have just given birth — which is often! We have moved more TVs, furniture, and household goods than Walmart on Black Friday.

A young mother in one of our missional communities once shared how she wanted to be able to have more time to serve others in the group and people in the neighborhood. Between Steph and her husband (who was a full-time student), they had three jobs and two little kids. There was just no time to do anything else. When asked what would help lighten her load and allow her to follow God's leading in this way, she said, "If I could give up my part-time job, I would be set. I'd have more time. But we're so broke that there is no way we could ever afford it."

"Okay, so what's the problem?"

The others in her missional community asked, "Well, how much do you make at that part-time job anyway?" She made about $400 a month, which wasn't much but was a lot when they were just getting by.

"Well, together we can pitch in and easily make up that money for you," they said. "We want you around more — no, we *need* you around more and on mission with us! What does everyone think?" Everyone agreed. So they collected the $400 each month, a small amount per person in this group of around sixteen or so, and gave it to Steph and her husband, Jim.

"I don't know if I can accept that," she said. "I don't deserve that; we don't deserve that." "Why not?" someone asked her. "If we truly believe the gospel, then we know that we never *deserve* God's grace — we can't earn it — but because of his great love and generosity, we have it. We can accept it or reject it. It's up to us."

Steph did believe the truth of the gospel, and the next day she quit her job and began to enjoy God's new blessing in her life and share it with others.

The night after this conversation, she posted on Facebook that she was quitting her job and that she was able to do that because her friends in community were paying what she used to make so that she would be freed up to serve God and others in a greater way.

The flood of responses allowed her to share the good news with many of her friends, who still could not believe it.

"It's true," she said. "That's how Jesus is; that's what life in his family is like."

SACRED SPACE

For several years now, we have organized community service days that we call Sacred Space. We borrowed this idea from our friends at Imago Dei Church in Portland, and it carries with it this idea that every thing and every place is just as sacred as the next. God's presence and his people make it so. Three or four times each year we pick something in one of our neighborhoods that is very much in need of repair or attention, and then we swarm that thing, serving our city with a display of the gospel of restoration.

Parks, community gardens, college campuses, homes, alleys, business districts, and more have all been transformed like one of those TV makeover shows. This has given us the opportunity to invite our neighbors to "walk in the ways of God" with us, but it also provides a great way to serve together as a family, not for our own benefit, but for the benefit of others to God's glory.

BUT SOMETIMES IT'S HARD ...

I have learned that just because we live as servants to others doesn't mean they are always happy or appreciative. This was magnified for me once on a very dangerous trip inside an active war zone in South Sudan. A group of us traveled into several villages and refugee camps to deliver 10,000 pounds of food we had shipped in with the help of local rebel troops who wanted to help us assist their people. The recipients were so poor and hungry they looked like walking stick people. These poor souls had not eaten in days or even weeks. Many were near death as they stood in endless lines waiting for unfortunately small rations from our supply of beans, rice, and other grains.

We had taken planes, trucks, boats, and more trucks through rivers, swamps, and war zones to get this food to them. And guess what?

They were not that thankful. Their needs were so great and our help so comparably small that they were angry there was not more. They knew that what we brought would soon run out again, which left them wondering what to do and what would happen next. I can still vividly remember desperate mothers with ballooned-belly babies clinging to their flat, pancake-like breasts begging me for more food. *Begging.*

Tears flow as I write this, not because of their anger, but because I cannot possibly imagine having to beg for food to save my baby's life.

These dear people, whom God loves, were not really mad at us. They were just losing hope. They did not know how they could possibly make these impossibly small supplies last until the next hoped-for relief.

One time I asked my friend Kevin, who had set up this trip, why he would possibly continue to go into these parts of the world and do these types of things. I'll never forget what he told me.

"Caesar," he said, "if these were my kids, I would sure hope that *someone* would."

"Whatever you do for the least of these. . . ."[4]

CLOSER TO HOME

Remember our friend Wanda whom we secured the new apartment for? Well, soon after we had moved her and her family and paid their security deposit and first three months' rent, she quit answering our calls. Not long after that her phone number changed. We tried stopping by a few times, but she would never answer the door.

Oh well. What can you do?

We had served her because we were called to, because we have been served and sent to serve. It affected our hearts. We were reminded of the great debt we owed God, and that Jesus came and paid every last dime for us — and how so, so many times we have "changed our number" and quit answering his calls. Yet God still wants to serve many others all over the world. And he wants to use us — his family — to do it.

THINGS TO THINK ABOUT

Are you quicker to ask for help or to give help to others? Why?

How/why is serving others such a strong display of the Good News?

How much of a servant are you? How would taking on the role of a servant change the way you interact with friends, parents, spouse (if you are married), children, neighbors, and coworkers?

When you don't "feel like" serving others, where do you go for strength and renewal?

How does knowing that you are now filled with the power that raised Christ from the dead (the Holy Spirit!) change your perspective?

Chapter 6

DISCIPLES

We are apprentices of Jesus who take responsibility for our own development and the growth of others.

DURING HIGH SCHOOL, one of my best friends was Brian Yee. As you may or may not guess from his last name, Brian's family is Chinese, and when Brian and I were growing up, their family business was our neighborhood laundry.

Brian lived upstairs above the laundry with his sister, parents, and grandmother, and from the time they were old enough to fold towels and sheets, Brian and his sister were expected to help with the workload. The Yees' business was a common model of how family-owned businesses were operated and staffed. All of life was a training and proving ground for the skills necessary to someday (his parents hoped) take over the family business — a classic apprenticeship model.

I loved hanging around Brian in the hustle and bustle of their busy laundry. The fresh, steamy smells of the washing and pressing machines mixed with the aroma of exotic foods their grandma always had simmering on the stove. Though they never really let me help much, I enjoyed being there and never forgot my experiences with them. When Tina and I started raising our children, we tried to integrate some of the same principles in the different businesses we owned and operated over the years.

One example was the large, formal banquet hall we owned, which my wife managed. After several months of hosting small business functions and parties, we decided to upgrade the capacity. Our first full-blown event was for five hundred people, a very formal graduation dinner. In some very unfortunate timing that we had not planned for, the new tables, chairs, plates, and silverware all showed up the same day of this large banquet.

Yikes!

Our daughter Justine, who was just five at the time, spent hours on her knees crawling around and stripping the shipping paper off two thousand chair legs. Christin, at seven years old, helped set formal service for five hundred — thousands of plates, glasses, and pieces of silverware! Our oldest, Little Caesar, who was nine and going on twenty, helped with a little bit of everything. When the guests started arriving, we dressed him in one of my tux shirts and a black bow tie and had him pouring water and clearing tables. He looked ridiculous in my oversized clothing, but he could not have been prouder to help! We also paid all the kids when they worked, and we helped them set up their own little budgets early in life and taught them how to steward their resources.

Obviously we weren't always that busy, but over the years our family owned several businesses, and our children were involved in all of them. In this way, they learned about life, hard work, and how to have fun while working. We learned how to manage their (and our) attitudes when we didn't feel like working or serving others, and we learned how to deal with people who were not pleased by our work or service to them. As our children matured, their roles changed, and so did our expectations of them as we saw and affirmed their gifts, skills, and growing character. All of this happened naturally as we helped one another, worked hard, ate, talked, laughed, and rested together.

As a family. Life on life.

Today my children are adults who have become incredibly generous people and hard workers. I believe it's because they were apprenticed — *discipled* — in all of life. But I'm not trying to give you some parenting plan to follow here. I'm trying to paint a picture of what being a disciple is like. A disciple is who we are, and *discipleship* is both taking responsibility to grow and taking responsibility for the growth and development of others. It is a matter of intentionality.

DISCIPLE OF WHOM?

Like most things in life, when it comes to our faith, we seem to be hardwired to think that we must *do* something in order to *be* someone. But I want us to pause for a moment and refocus on the reality that if we have put our hope and trust in Jesus, we have become a disciple of Jesus. That is part of our true identity.

A disciple is someone who has reoriented his or her life around another to become, in essence, who that person is. Sure, as always, who we are does lead to what we do and how we live, but at the heart of being a disciple of Jesus is a desire to be like him.

Someone who wants to know a lot about the Bible or even know a lot about Jesus is called a student. It is a good thing to gain knowledge of the Word, but we have to be careful, because knowledge can puff us up and lead us to think that because we know a lot we are therefore better than others. It can lead us to treat others as less than ourselves because we know more than they do.[1] But a person who wants to become one with Jesus and be transformed into his likeness is called a *disciple*.

As Ray Vander Laan says in *The Dust of the Rabbi*, "A disciple, more than anything else in the world, wants to *be* what the teacher *is*."[2]

If you were honest, would you say that more than anything else right now you are pursuing *being* a disciple of Jesus — having your heart and character transformed into the likeness of Jesus in every area of your life?

AS I AM YOU WILL BE

In the first century, when Jesus walked on this planet, being selected by a rabbi or teacher to follow him and become like him was considered a privilege and a rare honor. If a man exhibited a right heart and the motivation toward this process, he might be given the opportunity to "become like the master." If this happened, he took it as his responsibility to actively follow and learn and question and grow. It became the highest priority in his life.

The day you first believed, Jesus chose *you*. And he believes you can, in his strength and authority, become just like him. He said to his first disciples, "You did not choose me, but I chose you and appointed you so that you might go and bear fruit — fruit that will last."[3] And he still chooses and calls his followers today.

THIS CHANGES EVERYTHING

To fully look at our identity as a disciple requires us to back up a little. Remember, we are part of a family of missionaries sent as disciples who make disciples. The "mission" part of missionary assumes we are going on Jesus' mission, and there is only one mission Jesus ever gave the church: "Go and make disciples."[4]

Jesus never commanded us to hold elaborate worship services. He called us to follow him as a disciple and in turn make more disciples. Discipleship is about people becoming more like Jesus. It is the process of moving from unbelief to belief about who God is and what he has done in absolutely every area of life. An important part of living out our identity as a disciple is making more disciples.

I always thought that being a disciple meant taking a series of classes about life as a Christian — topics such as prayer, faith, obedience, and sin would all be covered, and discipling someone meant taking them through the same classes or topics I had been through. Maybe it would be a nine-week study, maybe something else, but you get the point.

But then I noticed some things in the Bible that Jesus said that rewired my thinking. I'm not sure how I missed this over the years, for I have read this passage many times, but seeing it anew changed everything for me: "If you hold to my teaching, you are really my disciples. Then you will know the truth, and the truth will set you free."[5]

Let's clarify what Jesus is saying here: walking in his ways and obeying his teachings is what it means to be his disciple — and this is what will lead us to know the truth, and that truth, in turn, will set us free.

Astounding. Did you notice the order? If a person lives as a disciple, walking in Jesus' ways, *then* they will come to know the truth that sets them free!

Then why have we so often done things in the *exact opposite* order with people? We have traditionally thought that if we could get a person to believe what we told them about Jesus, they would get set free, and *then* we would start discipling them. But this is not what Jesus said or how he modeled this concept. Jesus spent years with his disciples, none of whom were yet "Christians," leading them to walk in his ways and obey his teachings. Then, over time, they came to believe the truth about him and his Father, being set free from their sin and unbelief.

In Matthew 28:19, Jesus said, "Go and make disciples of all nations, baptizing them in the name of the Father and of the Son and of the Holy Spirit." Many scholars suggest this should sound more like the following: "As you go about your life, make disciples." This means we are called to invite others to walk in the ways of Jesus with us as we are living our everyday lives so that they will come to believe the gospel we proclaim and demonstrate by participating in Christ's life and community. Here they can repeatedly see and hear the gospel as it comes into contact with their normal lives.

The truth is that we are always in "discipleship" mode. Discipleship doesn't start after some "conversion" experience; it begins when we first meet someone and then invite them to begin to walk in God's ways.

The apostle Paul wrote, "So then, just as you received Christ Jesus as Lord, continue to live your lives in him, rooted and built up in him, strengthened in the faith as you were taught."[6] The same truths of the gospel that have set us free are also how we are now to grow and mature, becoming more like Jesus. We continue to walk in his ways with others in community, in regular life, comparing and contrasting gospel truth to any and every area of sin or unbelief in our lives. By doing this, we actually disciple others to faith in Jesus and then beyond toward maturity. That is what *being* a disciple is, and that is what *making* disciples looks like.

What is really amazing is to watch someone who has come to faith this way in community start to do the same with others. Their natural tendency is to invite those they love into this life with Jesus.

LATHER, RINSE, REPEAT

Justin was having a particularly rough day. He felt forgotten by God and disconnected from God's love. As if by a divine appointment, his dad came and knocked on the door to his bedroom. "Hey buddy, can I share a piece of Scripture with you? Check this out from Isaiah 49: 'Can a mother forget the baby at her breast and have no compassion on the child she has borne? Though she may forget, I will not forget you! See, I have engraved you on the palms of my hands.' "[7]

It was as if God had reached into Justin's room — into his heart — and encouraged him personally. "Thanks, Dad. You cannot imagine how much I needed to hear that today," said Justin.

While this might seem pretty cool, if not fairly normal for a parent to share the Word with his son, this encouraged Justin in an even profounder way. He had been an atheist growing up. His parents and family were what I call "Chreasters," people who go to church only on Christmas and Easter. He had no real familiarity with the Bible and did not believe in God or Jesus. He joined the US Marines at the age of nineteen and headed off to "be a man" and make a life of his own choosing. While on deployment in Afghanistan, he met a few Christians who were a part of his unit and became friends with them. Sitting together one night in a tent, suffering the 120-degree temperatures, the sounds of war and death echoing in the distance, another young corporal read something to him from the Bible.

> At just the right time, when we were still powerless, Christ died for the ungodly. Very rarely will anyone die for a righteous person, though for a good person someone might possibly dare to die. But God demonstrates his own love for us in this: While we were still sinners, Christ died for us.[8]

In that moment, Justin realized that he had *never* done something for another person simply out of love, without thought of how they might return the favor or how it might benefit him. His interactions with people had been purely transactional: *I do this for you. Now you do this for me. If you do this for me, then I will think highly of you.* And despite all of that, Jesus still came and died for *him.* He broke down in tears.

His friend led him to talk to God for the first time in a simple prayer, receiving forgiveness and asking God to give him a new heart that could truly love people. Justin accepted God's pursuit of him that night and began to seek Jesus' life over the plans that he had been making for himself.

DISCIPLES

Two years later, when Justin was finished with active duty in the Marine Corps, he returned home to Tacoma and moved back in with his parents. He was a new believer, and his enthusiasm and faith permeated every conversation. Pretty quickly he got connected with one of our missional communities, where he started living life like a local missionary with a group of young men and women. He learned how the gospel affected every aspect of his life as he served others and began to both receive and give unqualified, unconditional love.

Justin had saved up quite a lot of money while on deployment, and he started giving it away as he saw needs in our city. He paid for a homeless guy he met to get new tires on his car so the man could get to work without problems. He bought groceries for people begging for food on the street corner. One time he helped someone pay for a family member's funeral. His parents actually became annoyed with his level of generosity and told him that he had to be smart, that people were just using him. But they were noticing a profound change in Justin's life and heart. He was a different person than the one they had known when he was growing up, and Justin told them over and over how Jesus and the gospel were changing him.

Over time Justin's parents started to come to our Sunday gatherings with Justin and the rest of the Soma family. They felt comfortable with the casual environment (our gathering space is a large converted warehouse set up like a giant living room, with leather couches and chairs, coffee tables, rows of chairs where needed, and nonstop coffee and food), and they liked the way the "preacher" talked. They could understand what was being communicated, and that helped them to better understand what was happening in their son's life. It was at these gatherings that Justin's parents began to meet some of the others from his missional community, as well as some people closer to their own age who were in another group.

Justin suggested that they might enjoy having a meal with some of these people, and to his surprise they accepted. Over the next months, his parents began to see, taste, and experience the good news about Jesus in every area of their lives. They had time to get their questions answered, and they received loving encouragement to walk in light of the truth they were coming to believe. They were being transformed.

What amazes me about Justin's story is the natural, reproducible progression of things in his life. He first came to know and trust Jesus through a few faithful brothers in the military. They started him on the road of true faith, teaching him how to read the Bible and pray, but then his time in the service was over. Back home, God continued to disciple Justin in community. It was here that he began to mature and have an influence in others' lives, including his parents'. His words, actions, and repentance lived out before them had a profound impact on their understanding of who God is and how much he loved them.

They were discipled *to* faith in Jesus.

Justin's family had very naturally come to live among a community that lived out its faith in all of life. Christianity for them was not simply an hour or two on Sundays. His parents saw, heard, experienced, and participated in *true life* throughout the week and in every imaginable circumstance. The kingdom of God became real and tangible for them. They could see that the truth in the Word was real. They could see how it changes lives — and it changed theirs.

WHAT NEXT, LORD?

One of the hardest parts of being a disciple who makes disciples is figuring out whom exactly we are to be making into disciples. How do we naturally, in ways that don't freak people out or make us feel stupid, move into relationships in which we are helping people walk in the ways of Jesus so that they will come to know the truth that sets them free?

DISCIPLES

Let me share a simple process with you that I've come to call "What next, Lord?" Not too long ago, my wife, Tina, and I joined a few other friends who wanted to move beyond their weekly Bible study experience into living more like a family of missionaries.

We started out by having weekly barbecues together. One couple would host one week, and another the next. We went back and forth for several weeks. We handed out homemade flyers inviting people to come for a casual meal to "get to know their neighbors." Over time, as is always the case, we noticed natural relationships starting to develop with some of these new friends that seemed to come every week.

My wife quickly hit it off with a gal who grew up in the same city she did. I was becoming fast friends with a guy who also played guitar and loved riding motorcycles — Harleys to be specific. We found that while we didn't all instantly become superclose with everyone who came to our dinners, some people were definitely leaning into relationship. One of the women coming also worked in the same field as Sarah, a leader in our missional community, and they hit it off. That's how it went. Each of us naturally built friendships with one or two others. It seemed that God was giving us specific relational favor with a few.

We began to pray for these relationships, asking, "What next, Lord? What do you want us to do next, *specifically*, with each of these people you have brought into our lives?" We all felt that the Spirit spoke directly to our hearts the things we were to do next to develop these relationships and love our friends. It wasn't anything profound or crazy; it was stuff like, "Give Christy a call this week to see how that job interview went that she was nervous about." Or "Call Mike and see if he can pick you up from the airport when you return later this week." We shared what we believed we had heard from God and agreed to pray for one another that week — both for favor and that we would be obedient to our "What next?" opportunities.

99

We got together weekly to share how we each had followed through the previous week. Then we would pray again, "What next, Lord?" God did amazing things over the next several weeks. It seemed as if we were being divinely guided into "perfect" conversations and situations with these neighbors. I think we were. Our hope, and what we had asked God to guide us into relationally, was the opportunity to take some of our neighbors through the Story of God (more about that in chapter 7, and see appendix A). We ended up inviting seven of these people to join us as we went through the Story for the next ten weeks together. Six of them agreed. The one gal who wasn't ready to do that with us remained close to our circle of friends; it wasn't as if because she said no to joining us, we rejected her. She is still part of our community, and we love her. We still hope and pray for her to begin to "lean in" to deeper relationship with us and with Jesus, but for now she is where she is.

We saw God do great things over the next weeks and months, and we fell deeply in love with these new friends. God used his story and our lives together in community to help several come to faith in him as they began to walk in his ways together with us. And now we continue to pray for them, and for us, "What next, Lord?"

MANY HATS, SAME HEAD

Being a disciple is part of my identity, but my roles in life include being a father, husband, home owner, and so on. I don't leave behind my other roles when I focus on one of them; I am all of them, collectively, all the time, which means I will be going about all the normal stuff of my life, meeting my responsibilities *as a disciple*.

I have spent time weeding my gardens, painting my house, staining my deck, fixing plumbing leaks, and a bunch of other things as I've "discipled" folks in my community. We have spent countless hours together talking about every imaginable topic, much of it in light of our new gospel identity and what the Bible has to say about life, while working at everyday, ordinary things. We cannot truly see another person's heart and character while sitting in a series of classes or by just reading through materials together — but we can when we're all tired and there's more to be done. Many of these young folks need to develop the basic skills and practices necessary to be a husband, father, or mother someday, but they need to learn to do these things in light of being a disciple of Jesus. Discipling can be done at the same time, "as you go," giving discipleship a grounding in real life.

How many of us would see a plumbing project or watching kids together at the local playground as a *perfect* opportunity for discipleship?

Once I was having a more formal meeting with a young leader in our community, discussing some specific challenges he was facing in his leadership, when my teenage daughter interrupted us.

"Daddy, can I borrow the pickup truck to go help a friend move his couch?" she asked.

"Sure, sweetie," I replied. "But you'll need to check the oil in the truck first. It's been leaking lately."

"But I don't know how to do that, Dad."

I paused our meeting and asked this young brother to join me for a minute outside while I checked and added oil to the truck, and then gave my daughter some basic instructions on how to drive the old beast without getting herself or anyone else killed. She was blessed as she left to bless someone else. This leader was also shown that serving my daughter and making her a priority in that moment did not necessarily have to keep him from being discipled; in fact, as he was a young father too, it really moved his heart. He learned more from that few minutes of time spent helping my daughter than in the rest of our entire meeting.

I am a daddy, yes, but as a disciple who is always making disciples.

BUT SOMETIMES IT'S HARD ...

Many of us love the salvation part of being a Christian, having Jesus pay the price for our sins, not getting what our sinful life deserves, and avoiding eternal separation from God. But when it comes to being a disciple — well, that part hurts, like a stone being cut from a quarry where many parts need to be chipped off or busted loose. But through this process, a new shape emerges.

> "Listen to me, you who pursue righteousness
>   and who seek the LORD:
> Look to the rock from which you were cut
>   and to the quarry from which you were hewn;
> look to Abraham, your father,
>   and to Sarah, who gave you birth."[9]

I love the imagery here of being carved from a larger "legacy stone," which includes our forefathers and matriarchs of the faith who ultimately pointed to Jesus. God's design for how this happens is in community. He uses his Word and the influence of others as masons (some of whom are not very skilled yet) to bring forth the beauty of his Son in our lives and character.

Where does your heart go when someone in your life or community of faith brings a word of correction to you? Are you a teachable person, readily open to learning from others' experiences and insights? There will be many times in your life as a disciple that God will want and *need* to teach you things. Most likely he will use others to do that. He will use them to point out who he is, as found in his Word, and what is now true of you because of Jesus.

Will you be open to that?

A HARD QUESTION

In the book of John, not long after Jesus' resurrection, we read in chapter 21 of a beachside breakfast at which Jesus asks his disciple Peter over and over again, "Do you love me?" Peter answers each time, "You know that I love you!" And Jesus responds, "Then feed my sheep." Peter would have heard his Good Shepherd telling him, "Go and do what you have seen me do. As I have discipled and loved you, now show your love for me and others by going and making more disciples."

It seems a fair question to ask ourselves too. If we are not passionately pursuing Jesus as his disciples and in turn obediently making more disciples, do we — do you — really love Jesus?

There it is. The hard question.

Perhaps we love the forgiveness Jesus offers. Maybe we "signed up" for this Christianity thing to acquire for ourselves a "get-out-of-hell" card. But do we love the One who gave his life to provide all of this? It seems we can be more focused on our afterlife than on this present one, here today.

Will we turn our everyday lives over to God to remake them and us for his glory?

THINGS TO THINK ABOUT

Were you "apprenticed" in your faith as you became a Christian? Who showed you how to walk in Jesus' ways through all the areas of normal life?

If this has never happened, who might you begin to "do life" with as you grow in your discipleship?

Do you actively pursue your own spiritual growth and Christlikeness as the highest desire in your life?

Have you ever discipled anyone else in his or her walk with God? God will use you wherever you're at. Who might he have placed in your life that you can begin to disciple to faith in Jesus?

PART 3

RHYTHMS: HOW WE LIVE

WHEN I WAS A YOUNG BOY, there was a local television show for kids on each weekday morning called *The Ray Rayner Show*. Ray was like a best friend or that favorite uncle who showed up to play, showing cartoons and walking us through easy "do it yourself" craft projects. The sample project that had been prepared in advance as a model to work from always looked perfect. Ray's usually turned out a little messy and — well, less than perfect — kind of like the projects of those of us at home watching.

I loved it!

Ray wore a one-piece orange jumpsuit that had little square notes pinned all over it, notes to remind him of what came next in the show or to give him options for activities and things to do. No one episode was much different from the next, but these notes served as reminders nonetheless, making life easier and more enjoyable for Ray, his crew, and us out in television land.

As we'll see, God has given us natural reminders too — ways of engaging our new identity in the everyday rhythms of life. Once we notice them, it is hard not to see all of life filled with great opportunities for God's mission.

IT'S GOT A GOOD BEAT YOU CAN DANCE TO

After looking at how we live out our new identity, you could very well be thinking, *Whoa. If I were actually to begin to live out my true identity, my life would be filled with people — a lot. How would I ever make time for anyone else, let alone my own family and kids?* How do we have time to make new friendships that lead to discipleship?

Everything in *my* life pulls me to want to set *my* schedule to do *my* stuff when I want it done — for *my* pleasure, fitting *my* priorities.

It's normal to feel some tension related to laying down your life for others. You have been living in certain patterns for years, so it isn't always immediately clear how to live out a missional life day by day. I want to suggest that the secret to increasingly living our lives on Jesus' mission is to move from seeing disciple making as something additional that needs to be tacked onto life toward seeing all the normal stuff and rhythms of life as full of opportunity for discipleship and growth in the gospel. We need only to fill these rhythms with greater gospel intentionality. We must move from an *additional* mind-set to an *intentional* mind-set[1] in the normal patterns of life that God has given us. As the apostle Paul exhorts, "Be very careful, then, how you live — not as unwise but as wise, making the most of every opportunity, because the days are evil."[2]

As we continue, I'll share with you six rhythms — *story-formed, listen, eat, bless, celebrate,* and *re-create* — that happen over and over again in every city, neighborhood, and village in the world.[3] I have found that being aware of these rhythms helps me see all the normal routines of life as easy opportunities for living out my gospel identity and inviting others to walk in the ways of Jesus. Like Ray Rayner's notes pinned to his jumpsuit, let them serve as reminders of how a normal life can be filled with God's good news as we turn our focus even further outward. These rhythms have helped many to see and proclaim God in the mundane, the spectacular, the seemingly unimportant, and the critical parts of daily life.

You may already be living in these rhythms and never noticed.

Chapter 7

STORY-FORMED

*We understand, experience, and intersect with
God's story and the stories of others.*

THE HIT MOVIE *My Big Fat Greek Wedding* is the story of Fotoula
"Toula" Portokalos, who at thirty years old is the only woman in her
family who has failed to get a man. Everyone expects her to marry
a Greek boy, make Greek babies, and feed everyone until the day
she dies. But Toula feels trapped working in the family restaurant,
Dancing Zorba's, and lives her life under the constant scrutiny and
comparisons of her parents, siblings, and pretty much everyone in
her life as she pursues her own path. The movie is a hilarious picture of life in a Greek family. Every time my wife and I watch it, we
can't help but laugh. Now, we're not Greek, and no one in my family knows how to make souvlaki, but wait — is this my family too?

My dad doesn't spray Windex on his rashes, as Toula's father did
in the movie, but he did once put black, greasy shoe polish on the
back of his head to cover a spot where he cut his own hair down
to the scalp.

That *really* happened — come on, Dad!

Our lives are wrapped up in stories; they are the language of
our world. We hear a good, powerful story and we relate; we're

implicated, affirmed, and changed by listening and participating in the story. Think about your favorite movies or books and how they draw you in. You begin to feel what the characters feel, their pain becomes your pain, and their victory becomes your victory. Stories are the most powerful form of communication we have; they speak to our minds and to our emotions, and they can even affect us physically.

And everyone everywhere has a story.

FLANNELGRAPH THEOLOGY

I grew up going to Sunday school pretty much every week of my young life. Our teachers told us amazing stories from the Bible, nicely illustrated with flannel characters, all of them ending with a nice moral, such as, "If you have faith like David had, you can slay any giant in your own life too!" Or "So, kids, if you're obedient like Noah, God will protect you from all the bad stuff in your life."

Not only did those teachers miss the point of the stories (God is always the hero!), but they never taught us that the Bible is one *big* story. In fact, it is the *Story of God*. It's not a collection of unrelated moralistic tales, nor is it a history lesson. The Bible tells a living and active story that is still unfolding — and we are characters in this story!

Imagine you are trying to put together a 10,000-piece jigsaw puzzle. You have to put in a lot of time and work to get to the point where you can actually see the picture the artist intended. But think about how difficult your task would be if you did not have the lid to the puzzle box with a picture of the completed puzzle. You would have no way to tell what exactly you were trying to piece together.

"Is this a part of the sky or a reflection of the lake? Is this animal fur or a piece of a tree?"

For many of us, this is how we have learned the Bible. It mirrors the process we've engaged in to grow in our faith and understanding of who God is and what he is doing. We have heard sermon after sermon and have done one book study after another without really knowing what the big picture of this whole "Christianity thing" really is. Every once in a while, we'll fit a couple of pieces together and rejoice. And some of us have been around church and the Bible long enough to have all of the "edge pieces" put together, the basic framework of the Bible, but we still do not really know the Bible as one big story. We are not superclear on who exactly God is, what he has done, who we are in light of this, and how we should live.

We do not know the Story of God.

SHAPED BY THE STORY OF GOD

Is the story that most shapes your life and identity the Story of God that is told throughout the Bible? Or is it a story from your culture, dysfunctional background, or a stack of lies that makes up the primary narrative of your life? Because who we believe ourselves to be is shaped by the dominant story in our lives, and what we believe about God and what he is like will ultimately determine what we believe about ourselves and how life works.

Let me share with you how God used his story being told, discussed, and prayed over in our community to forever change the life of one of my dear friends.

Railene grew up in a home where God was talked about "a little," usually around Christmas and Easter, sometimes when someone was sick, but not a whole lot otherwise. She knew that "Jesus died for her sins," but other than that, she had no real understanding of who God is and how much he cares for her. In junior high she started hanging out with a local church youth group and quickly joined the choir and pretty much anything else she could get involved in.

She was the "good girl" and proud of it. But today Railene would tell you she was wearing a well-crafted mask, not allowing anyone to see who she really was.

"There was a lot I didn't know about God," she said. "But I never invested time and energy in learning the things I needed to know. I never asked questions because by the time I realized I needed answers, I felt I couldn't ask them. I should already have known this stuff! I was afraid of looking stupid."

After high school, Railene started dating the man who would become her husband. Jason was the son of a pastor and the man of her dreams, a gentle guy who loved Jesus and loved Railene, and the two began to plan a life together. During their engagement, however, Jason started seeing a side of Railene he (and others) had never seen before: intense anger. They began to fight a lot.

"Not only was there anger, but there was an insane amount of guilt in my life over some past sins. I would feel guilty for something, then angry, then guilty for the anger, then angry again. It was this never-ending cycle that I felt helpless in."

The two got married and started having kids, and the cycle of anger, guilt, and shame only grew worse. Eventually, turning her anger at God, Railene stopped going to church, hanging out with Christians, and talking about her faith. She totally avoided all things Christian. She wondered why God wouldn't take her bitter feelings away, and she quickly spiraled into a deep depression. *Does God even love me?* she would wonder.

A bunch of us from my missional community, including Jason (without Railene), were getting together a lot, and we decided that since the weather was nice, we would spend several weeks going through the Story of God together. We sat on my deck overlooking my backyard and my beloved Northwest palm trees. We ate simple but great food together. Some folks shared a bottle of wine.

It was all a very relaxed and normal "hanging out" time for folks in Tacoma. In an amazing answer to Jason's prayers, he invited Railene to join us for this "story time," and she accepted! (For a summary of the story we went through, see appendix A.)

Railene began to ask a lot of questions, really engaging in the dialogue we were having as we went through God's story. She asked questions with the inquisitiveness of a child — truly wanting to know — and then as we talked about what we learned from the story, she had some very profound insights. She encountered a community that was there for her, and she felt free and safe to open up and be herself, to get answers to questions she never dared ask before about the Bible and God.

Most importantly, she was truly coming alive.

This led Railene to be open to coming to our Sunday gatherings, where she met others who eventually helped lead her out of her anger and shame and into the arms of Truth. She learned along the way that she never needed to hide from God; in fact, she couldn't. He was right there with her all along, and he loved her and was not put off by her anger or questions. God is crazy about Railene and has much he wants to show her as he continues to write her story.

FIRST THINGS FIRST

I had just moved out to Tacoma and was sharing this Story of God for the first time there with a group of leaders involved in ministry. After telling just the first few short narratives, I asked them a question: "What are you seeing differently now, or for the first time, after listening to and discussing just this much of the Story of God?" A seventy-year-old saint who had been serving the church faithfully for more than fifty years said, "For the first time in my life, I am seeing the Bible as a story about a God who is pursuing and loving *me*! He's not waiting to scold me or shame me for my sins.

He is brokenhearted by my sin, but he is patient and forgiving. And he loves *me*."

This is why we start our missional communities by telling and experiencing the Story of God together. Along the way, over the weeks we spend with one another going through this chronological narrative, we also tell our own stories and find the similarities and overlap between us and God and all other humans throughout history. The questions we address are not your normal Bible study quiz show stuff; they help illuminate who God is and what he desires for his people.

We speak into one another's lives with care and Spirit-led insight. The storyteller does not act as teacher, but rather as guide, leading people back to God's story for their answers and insights. This is not a matter of the blind leading the blind or a "pooling of ignorance"; this is a divinely led process that has the power to transform lives. We come to understand God's heart and what really lies hidden in our own hearts. These times of food, drink, laughter — and sometimes tears — have marked us like nothing else ever has.

I am often asked, "What is the one main thing that has changed your understanding of what it means to be a Christian?" It is this. God's story has implicated us, and now we understand why we exist, who we are, and how we *get to* live.

ARE YOU STORY-FORMED?

How much have you been shaped by stories, and by God's story, when it comes to living out your faith?

> Do you know the overarching themes and story of the Bible?
> Do you know the stories of those in your community or
>   circle of close friends? Do you know their stories with
>   enough detail and history to understand their needs
>   and really bear with them?

Do you know the story of your neighborhood or city? What are the "pain points" and long-standing idols of the people, collectively?

Do you spend time getting to know your neighbors' stories and sharing yours with them?

Will you invite others into God's story?

APOSTLES' FEET AND TEMPLE COURTS

"Lord! What an absolutely amazing evening this was! I feel as if we were transported, in answer to our prayers, back to the times of the book of Acts. I just knew you meant what you said in that book, that the essence of all that continually took place in the early church was real then and could be real today."

Our experiment in telling the Bible story in public began as an attempt to rewire our thoughts as a community on what "not giving up meeting together" means.[1] When, where, why, and how did the early church gather when they got together? Were there clues to be found in the Bible? Could God still be writing his story now in similar yet entirely new ways?

In the book of Acts, Luke gives us some clues about how the early church lived in community.

> They devoted themselves to the apostles' teaching and to fellowship, to the breaking of bread and to prayer. Everyone was filled with awe at the many wonders and signs performed by the apostles. All the believers were together and had everything in common. They sold property and possessions to give to anyone who had need. Every day they continued to meet together in the temple courts. They broke bread in their homes and ate together with glad and sincere hearts, praising God and enjoying the favor of all the people. And the Lord added to their number daily those who were being saved.[2]

Awesome! I wanted all of that.

I was especially drawn to the "they devoted themselves to the apostles' teaching ... and hung out together as they met in homes" part. We were doing that together. Check. But I was a little unsure about the part that says, "Every day they continued to meet together in the temple courts." How would we do that part? What are our "temple courts" today?

After the Jews of the day were finished with their official sacrificial business at the temple in Jerusalem, they would often hang out and barter, trade, and shoot the breeze for a while in the court-yard surrounding the temple. For us in Tacoma, the modern-day equivalent is our cafés and pubs. That is where everyone hangs out with no particular agenda.

So we found a place that would allow us to host a "Storytelling Night." The Kickstand is a local hipster café where angst-ridden teens and pierced and tattooed twentysomethings mingle with poets, artists, and middle-aged wannabes. Our hope was that our storytelling night could be a time of interaction with not-yet believers when we told the Story of God in a modern "temple court." Could we bring the kingdom to the people in our city instead of waiting for them to find it somehow?

That's what happened.

We tacked up a few posters around town, ran blurbs in the local-scene mags, and started inviting people to "bring a story, bring a friend" on Tuesday evenings. Surprisingly, people showed up. As the weeks went by, more showed up. And then a lot of people jammed into this little café to participate in the experience.

I was the host for these events and would start off each night laying a couple of ground rules. I let everyone know that we wanted this to be a time of community and respect, and that as different people told their stories, the audience would be allowed to ask questions and the presenters could ask them questions in return; we wanted to engage in a dialogue. "This is a practice I learned while on a trip to Africa," I told them.

They loved this idea!

I would start the night off with a simple, usually funny story and then pose a few questions to get things going. Then I would ask, "Who else has a story to tell?" As the night progressed, we were treated to the widest array of humor, pain, creativity, vulgarity, and just plain weirdness that you could ever imagine. Some folks read poetry; others told parts of their own life stories. Along the way, I would eventually get up and say, "Okay, I have another story to tell tonight." I usually told three or four different stories each week, but only one was the next story told chronologically in the Story of God.

"This is a story found in the bestselling book in human history — the Bible. A lot of people think it's a true story, a lot of people don't. I happen to believe it's true, but wherever you're at, just like we've done all night, after I'm finished I'll ask a few questions, and you can ask me any questions that come to mind."

People had such different perspectives and insights. I heard things I never would have heard on a million Sundays in church but that shaped my faith forever. We became friends, and several became part of our community on mission. Many of us started hanging out together and became lifelong friends. You would have had to be there to fully understand what we experienced over those twenty-five weeks together.

We felt God affirming this new "incarnation" of his Son and our obedience to his call to live in a new kingdom rhythm of life. As God's story unfolded, our stories gained meaning. We saw and experienced the heart of God being revealed in this dingy little café as we sipped coffee, listened, and learned. Our little experiment to "gather in the temple courts" had become a beautiful display of the kingdom of God, as people from all walks of life were shaped and formed by the story they heard.

TO BE KNOWN

Everyone has a story. Put another way, everyone's life is a story,[3] and it is amazing to watch someone tell their story. They may start out slow, feeling a little intimidated and unsure at first, but as they get going something remarkable happens. I have seen people change before my eyes as they've told their story in community. For some, it is the first time anyone has really listened to them and heard their heart's cry, really giving them the space and time to just be.

As the family of God, we have an awesome gift and responsibility. When we listen to others speak, it's as if God himself is sitting there listening to them, for we are now the body of Christ — and that includes his ears!

When people feel that God knows them — and still chooses to love and accept them regardless of their past sin, pain, or running away from him — something shifts. Trust begins to grow. This is why it is so important to take the time to get to know the stories of your friends and neighbors, those whom God has sent you on a rescue mission to scoop up and bring back home.

The apostle Paul asked some new believers, "So now that you know God (or should I say, now that God knows you), why do you want to go back again and become slaves once more to the weak and useless spiritual principles of this world?"[4] It is no small thing for any of us to be known by God. Can you imagine if you actually got to hang out with Jesus, and he knew you and actually liked you? Remember, he's God, so he would *really* know you — and all your stuff. You might feel a little like a woman Jesus met one day while getting water at a well.[5] A poem based on that passage lets us in on what she must have felt.

To be known is to be loved;
And to be loved is to be known.
And I just met you.
But I love you.
I don't know you,
but I want to get to.
Let me run back to town
this is way too much for just me.
There are others: brothers,
sisters, lovers, haters.

The good and the bad, sinners and saints
who should hear what you've told me;
who should see what you've shown me;
who should taste what you gave me;
who should feel how you forgave me.

For to be known is to be loved;
And to be loved is to be known.[6]

BUT SOMETIMES IT'S HARD ...

Teaching people God's story can be difficult at times, especially with those who feel they already have a strong knowledge of the Bible and Christianity. They can sit as gatekeepers, waiting to find any discrepancy or idea they disagree with. My experience after sharing the Story of God hundreds of times around the world with thousands of people is that few people truly know the story found in the Bible. They know pieces of it, but few understand the overarching story.

I once told God's story to a group of folks who were starting missional communities in their city, and one of their team members sat directly in front of me with a big, four-inch-thick copy of the Bible in Greek! "I prefer to study it in the original language," he said.

Yikes.

Every so often while I was telling the Story, he would wrinkle up his face as if he had just smelled something rotten, and dive into his massive Holy Book to see if what he had just heard was accurate. After reading a bit, he would jut out his bottom lip, nod slightly in agreement, and return to listening. I think I lost ten pounds of sweat that day. Fortunately, he never found anything in the Story that he disagreed with.

Get ready. Because teaching people who think they already know everything can be hard.

BUT WHEN ARE WE GOING TO GO DEEPER?

For years Christians have sat in endless Bible studies with little life change. The knowledge they have acquired has produced scarce fruit in them. The Bible itself teaches that knowledge alone is of little value; in fact, as I mentioned earlier, it can puff us up and trick us into thinking we have "arrived" in our faith. Jesus himself said, "You have your heads in your Bibles constantly because you think you'll find eternal life there. But you miss the forest for the trees. These Scriptures are all about *me*! And here I am, standing right before you, and you aren't willing to receive from me the life you say you want."[7]

It is one thing to know a lot *about* God and the Bible; it is another to understand and experience his loving pursuit as seen throughout all of Scripture. Sharing the good news about Jesus and his kingdom through the lens of facts and topics can become cold and clinical. But there is nothing more moving than having the ability to easily and naturally share the Story of God. It is the most transforming thing we can give ourselves to, and it is the one thing that I have seen consistently move people from unbelief to belief and trust in God. There is nothing *deeper* than knowing, experiencing, hearing, and obeying God's Word as found in the Story.

What you think about God will define who you believe yourself to be.

LIVE AS AN APPETIZER

Our lives in Christ now are but a foretaste of what is yet to come in fullness. Our new, transformed stories, lived out in community, should give people a glimpse of what heaven is like.

Salvation is not just about *someday*. It is about *this day*.

The Bible is not a story about how jacked up we are, and the Good News is not a message about how we can evacuate this broken world with our souls. Our faith, the Story, Christianity — these all bring hope rooted not in escape or evacuation, but in participation and restoration. This is not a story about leaving; it is about staying, proclaiming, and renewing!

Each of our stories is being rewritten, and together our stories are being woven together into a beautiful and multicolored tapestry of grace and mercy, giving hope to others that this good news just might be true for them, that maybe there is a transformation waiting to happen to them too.

Our story of people very unlike one another becoming a family gives hope to those watching — that perhaps there is a place for them too.

Our stories of how Jesus has served us, and how we now get to serve one another, give hope that there is help.

Our stories of how God sent his Son on a rescue mission and found us, saved us, and transformed us give hope to the lost that maybe someone is out there looking for them too.

Together we are a living testament that is still being written.

The Story continues with us.

THINGS TO THINK ABOUT

What sticks out to you after reading the short summary narrative of the Story of God in appendix A?

What did you learn about God from this? What did you learn about Jesus?

Do you think most people you know have heard and understood this basic yet powerful story? How do you think most people view the Bible?

What would change if more and more people had the opportunity to listen to and engage God's story in meaningful ways in a safe, shared environment?

Pray and ask God who he would want you to share his story with.

Chapter 8

LISTEN

We set aside regular times to listen to God —
both backward and forward.

MY FRIEND JAYNE did a graphic design project for a friend at work. It was nothing official, just something Greg needed done personally, and he promised to pay her $100 for the work once completed. After she finished it, a few months went by, but Greg forgot to pay her the money.

Jayne prayed and told God, "I want this $100, Lord. I have stuff I want to do and spend that money on." She heard God in prayer say back to her, "I am going to take care of that, and when I do, I want you to send that money to your friend Debbie." Well, you'd have to know this sister Jayne — she speaks very frankly to God at times, and she told him, "I will do that Lord, but you'll have to give me that money today; otherwise, if it comes later, I am going to spend it on myself."

Pretty bold.

Amazingly, when Jayne went to work that day, opened up the door to her office, and flipped on the lights, there was a check from Greg for $100 on her desk.

Shoot, Lord, Jayne thought. *Did I really say this?* Quickly, before her desire for that cute little jacket she had her eye on got the best of her, she mailed the check off to Debbie, who lived in another city, along with a note explaining that the Lord had told her that she was supposed to send this money. Jayne was filled with an odd sense of joy afterward, knowing that whatever happened, she had acted in obedience and that was all that mattered.

A couple of weeks later, Jayne got a card back from Debbie, whose words were jumping off the page as she thanked Jayne for listening to their caring and loving heavenly Daddy. She explained that God was teaching her and her husband about tithing, and they were learning to trust him for their finances and provision. The tithe check they had written to their church in faith a couple of weeks earlier had bounced, along with a few other checks they had sent out that month. The bank fees to cover the bounced checks were $90. When Debbie received the money Jayne sent her, she was able to pay the $90, leaving her $10 — to tithe on the $100 gift!

Debbie and her husband cried that day. They couldn't believe God cared so deeply for them, enough to speak to Jayne thousands of miles away, and they grew in their faith that God would continue to provide for their needs. Jayne also wept that day, comforted by the fact that her God listens, still speaks, and is not put off in the least by her being completely real with him.

TURN DOWN THAT NOISE!

Would you say that your life is prioritized for listening to God? Busyness, phone calls, texts, tweets, Facebook updates, uploads, and downloads — our days and lives are crammed full of noise. A deep crackling distortion fills us at a soul level. Perhaps some of us keep our ears and hearts full of noise because deep down inside we are afraid of what we might hear God say.

But we have nothing to fear.

Jesus regularly listened to God in prayer so he would know his Father's will. We are also called to listen to God in prayer, but this differs from a prayer life that has us doing all the talking. We can listen *backward* by regularly interacting with God's Word, and we can also spend time actively listening *forward* to his Spirit and to him through our community. I am not trying to give a lesson on prayer here, at least not in the way prayer is usually taught, the "quiet time" kind of prayer. I want to look at the difference between a prayer life that has us treating God like a magic genie, frantically giving God our sanctified to-do list, and a life of listening to God speak in real time with a new rhythm as part of our day-to-day life.

LISTENING BACKWARD

How often do you read the Bible? (It is a book from God — amazing!) Are you listening for God to speak when you read his words? What is God saying and what will you do with what he says? Are you listening for the Word to take on flesh?

God's story is a movement from Word to flesh, and things should change in your world after experiencing the Word. A friend of mine asks himself (and others) these three simple questions after reading from the Bible:

What is God saying to you?
What do you think he wants you to do about it?
Who else in your life would benefit from hearing this too? Go tell them.

These simple steps can make a big difference immediately, and doing them reflects the heart of a servant ready to listen and obey.

LISTENING FORWARD

Look at how Jesus prayed and listened, and notice the context, frequency, and reason for his prayers:

"I do nothing on my own but speak just what the Father has taught me. The one who sent me is with me; he has not left me alone, for I always do what pleases him."[1]

Jesus did and said *nothing* without checking in with our Dad first. He must have been listening constantly. He was and is God himself, but only after listening did he act and speak. Notice the parallel in Jesus' words to his disciples right before he left to go back to his Father:

"All authority in heaven and on earth has been given to me. Therefore go and make disciples of all nations. . . . And surely I am with you always, to the very end of the age."[2]

If Jesus is with us always, then we should be listening to him speak. Imagine how different your decisions, actions, and words could all be if you were to cultivate a rhythm of checking in with Jesus first. A lot. You *get* to.

ARE YOU LISTENING TO ME?

As I am writing this chapter today, our national elections are going on. For the past few months, I have listened to countless arguments, brags, accusations, and promises being made by both the Democrats and Republicans. To be honest with you, it has all started to sound pretty much the same to me. Every candidate is for better education, safer streets, and creating new laws to protect citizens. Of course, who doesn't want all of that? Who is correct? Which candidate should I trust? Which should I listen to?

We are always listening to someone, always choosing what to believe and then acting on those beliefs. Every day we all pretty much do what we want to do based on what we have heard and believe — even if it is coming from within our own heads and desires. Whom we listen to and place our trust in is a big deal.

One day in the garden, Adam and Eve chose to listen to a voice other than God's. They listened to what the serpent said to them and acted on it. They chose to believe that they could do a better job of managing good and evil, right and wrong for themselves. But God had warned them that when they "ate from that tree," they would die.[3]

As humans, we were never created to manage the choices about right and wrong alone for ourselves. We were made to walk closely with God, listening to his voice and trusting his decisions to bless our lives and bring glory to him.

God is alive. He is speaking all the time.

Are you willing to listen?

LISTENING *IS* DOING SOMETHING

There is a great guy in our community who moved from Chicago to Tacoma with my family when we first came to start Soma. William is full of life and a true servant in every sense of the word. I love this guy, and I love his heart.

There is also a young woman in our community whom William had met a few times — no sparks though — until one day when he saw Bre dressed as Raggedy Ann for a costume party. Whoa! Something in his heart shifted. In that moment, he felt like God told him, "Pursue that woman." Really?

Really.

"So how do I do that?" he asked God.

The Spirit told him to be a servant and good brother to her. Over the next few months, he served her in any way he could. When she broke her leg and was laid up for months, William brought meals to Bre eight times. He brought her laundry to fold (she asked for it; she loves to fold laundry), rented movies for her to watch, and just spent time *being* with her. He was the best friend and brother to her he knew how to be. There was no talk of dating; he just served her.

And he kept listening.

The leaders in Bre's missional community saw how William was pursuing her honorably and asked if he was still hoping to start officially dating her. He let them know that he was but that he was waiting for God to give him the go-ahead. They suggested that he wait to ask her out until she was off the pain medication she was taking for her leg injury. They wanted her to be clearheaded and fully present if William were to ask her out. A few weeks later, Bre was off her meds and William knew the time had arrived. Mustering up his courage and charm, William asked Bre out on a date sometime, and she gave him a nice, long, kindly worded response that amounted to a *big fat no*.

Ouch.

It was not what Willy had hoped to hear. But he was still sure that he and others in the community had heard the Spirit clearly. Bre told me that William continued to do things for her that felt like he was pursuing her, though from William's perspective, it felt like a regression in their relationship.

Then, on a Sunday morning at one of our larger gatherings, he heard a message on what the Bible has to say about our trust and love for God in connection with pursuing and caring for a woman. There were some hard words between him and the Spirit after that. For two days he wrestled with God and with his own heart over what he had heard. God wanted Willy to love and trust him more than he desired to have Bre in his life. Sitting in his car, he prayed, "I know you want me to release Bre to you, but I am just not ready to do it. I really want to have her, to marry her. You'll have to change my heart in this."

The Holy Spirit gently led him to repent, to change his mind and believe the truth. He began to truly believe that God was good and satisfying and would be there perfectly forever for him, regardless of when and if things ever worked out with this woman.

Two minutes later — no kidding — a friend texted William and said that he and his wife were going to dinner and dancing that weekend, and they wanted to know if he wanted to bring a date and join them. He thought, *I have to call and ask Bre!*

But naturally William was a little afraid that she was going to turn him down again. "I know I have to release Bre and this situation to you, Lord," he prayed, "but I really want her! You'll work this out, right?"

God spoke back to Willy, saying, *You are only willing to release her to me if things work out the way you want them to. That's not trust. Releasing something or someone into my hands means being okay with what I choose to do with it.*

William told me, "I was afraid to ask her out again, but I knew I *had* to ask her in faith, to be in a position of trusting God. If I didn't ask her out because of fear, I would be continuing to trust in me and my timing, not in God and what he said."

Later that day, mustering up all the faith he had, and remembering what he had heard God speak to him, he called Bre to ask her out to dinner and dancing.

Push the pause button a second!

Bre also heard God speak to her that day: *William is going to ask you out again.* She told God, "But you know, Lord, that I don't have those kinds of feelings for him right now." Yet she felt like God was asking her to go ahead and say yes, accepting his pursuit. Afterward, while just starting to share all of this with a friend, the phone rang. She hadn't even gotten to the part about William yet — and it was William!

And in obedience to what she heard God saying, she said, "Yes, dinner and dancing would be great."

William melted.

Now, I know Willy pretty well, and he is talented at a lot of things, but he is not the best dancer. The evening went great anyway, and he was able to open up to Bre and to God that night in ways he had not been able to before. Bre later told him that God had been telling her to accept his pursuit. Obviously God was at work in both their hearts, working out something for his glory.

Thanks, Dad!

William and Bre started hanging out a lot more after that night and officially became "a couple" a month later. It was fun to see the photos posted on Facebook of them out hiking or together at parties. They dated for several months, but God has since put the brakes on that part of their relationship as he continues to speak to their hearts, to their humanness. They're both learning that they need to listen more and act less — to look for how God wants to grow their trust in him and his plans as he prepares them for a future of his choosing.

This story is still being written, but it is one that has God's handiwork all over it.

Listening to God can be hard, but it shows a posture of humility. It says that what God has to say is more important than anyone or anything else, including me and my thoughts or opinions, which are so easily tossed around by the stress of the day, someone's negative comments, or past experiences.

> My child, listen to what I say,
>> and treasure my commands.
> Tune your ears to wisdom,
>> and concentrate on understanding.

Cry out for insight,
    and ask for understanding.
Search for them as you would for silver;
    seek them like hidden treasures.
Then you will understand what it means to fear the LORD,
    and you will gain knowledge of God.[4]

DIRECT CONNECTION

Nowadays we have amazing Batman movies, but when I was a kid we had the cheesy TV Batman. Commissioner Gordon had a red telephone on his desk — no dial or keypad — just a single black button that, when pushed, dialed up Batman directly.

Spoiler alert! It actually called Bruce Wayne.

With 24/7 access to Batman, why *wouldn't* you use a phone like that when times got tough?

Prayer and listening is a little like that. Not only are we able to bring our needs and concerns to God, but we can call anytime and God will speak. Sometimes he speaks, *Wait*; sometimes he gives comfort or direction; but we have a direct line to the throne of God at all times!

Why don't we use it more often?

I am trying to cultivate a rhythm of going away on set-aside days of solitude, where I do nothing but listen for what God wants to tell me. I bring my Bible, a notepad, or sometimes my laptop for taking notes, but I turn off all media and disconnect from the Internet for a day or two and just listen and converse with God. At first this was really, really hard for me. It took hours, if not days, it seemed, just to turn down the noise in my head. But with patience and practice, I am coming to know how to sit in the presence of God, waiting on his voice. God has never failed to meet me in these times, usually pointing out a few things about my life and attitude that he wants to work on, but always speaking lovingly and gently to my soul.

A few years ago, on one of these breaks, I started by asking God a question related to my life and ministry. I was in a position at our church that was perfectly suited to my gifts and abilities. I was working with people I loved. But God had been causing something in my heart to shift, and I sensed he was waiting to say something.

"I love what I'm doing, Father. You have been so good to me and my family. In some ways, I feel ungrateful for even asking, but should I stay here, or are you releasing me?"

As I walked along the river that gray fall afternoon, I heard God say, almost audibly it seemed, *I am releasing you.*

"To where, Lord?"

You already know the place.

Well, that place turned out to be Tacoma, and our move here six months later began what has become the greatest adventure of my life as God has led us to live like a family of missionary servants and help others do the same.

I am very glad that God and I had that conversation. It taught me to listen. It showed me I could trust what I heard, and it caused me to desire to live my life in real-time listening mode. Writing this book is a real-time conversation with God. I want to say only what he tells me to say. In conversations with others, I am cultivating a "listening ear" that is trying to discern the Spirit as I talk with others. *What is he saying? What should I say or not say?* At times when I am in meetings I will ask, "Would it be okay if we just stopped for a minute and asked God for his wisdom, direction, and timing in all of this?" God usually speaks in those moments.

BUT SOMETIMES IT'S HARD ...

I have a confession to make. Even though I am learning to listen, my natural spiritual rhythm has never been that prayerful. Maybe you can relate to this. I've learned that I need to prioritize this rhythm in my life like anything else I do regularly that is important, such as going to work Monday through Friday or going to the gym a few times each week. If it's important, I schedule it in. Why not schedule times to intentionally listen to God?

Trying to tell others that you have heard from God on their behalf can seem weird or even manipulative. How is someone supposed to respond when we say, "God told me to tell you this"? So make sure to talk to God about people more than you talk to the people directly. Be sure your heart is in a position of advocating for them.

People have often asked me how they can know when God is speaking, and my response is that hearing from God always produces the fruit of the Spirit — love, joy, peace, forbearance, kindness, goodness, faithfulness, gentleness, and self-control — in our hearts and lives, as well as a sense of assuredness.

Is this what you are sensing in your heart after listening to God?

Also, what you hear will always be in line with Scripture. This is how knowing God's Word — listening backward — connects with listening forward. You must know his Word in order to know if what you are hearing lines up with what God has said and done in the past.

When I'm in a tense situation and I feel that little defensive, self-protective knot starting to form in my heart, I go after it with Jesus. "What is this going on in my heart, Lord?" I turn my thoughts into prayers, into a conversation with God, telling him my feelings, anger, and fear. Then I pause to hear how he responds.

I am learning to notice that little changes in my attitude, unexpected pauses, or a surprising shift in my day may be a cue that God wants to speak with me. Sometimes I'll wake up in the middle of the night or very early in the morning with the strongest sense that God either wants me to pray for someone or wants to tell me something. I have had to cultivate this rhythm over time, learning to push out the noise in my life and tune in to God's still small voice.

When I feel pretty certain that I have heard God's voice, I move toward it. Sometimes I trip, but it's better to try to listen and obey (even when wrong) than to fail to act in faith and do nothing.

BUT WAIT, THERE'S MORE!

Some believe that all we need in order to know God's will is the Bible, that everything he wanted to reveal to us is in there. Period. But God has more that he wants to say, more that he wants to teach us. He didn't say it when he was on the earth, because apparently the disciples couldn't handle it yet. He said that he would reveal these things through his Spirit.

> "I have much more to say to you, more than you can now bear. But when he, the Spirit of truth, comes, he will guide you into all the truth. He will not speak on his own; he will speak only what he hears, and he will tell you what is yet to come."[5]

We must be listening in order to hear all that Jesus has for us, all that God wants for us. That is the role of the Holy Spirit in our lives. Remember, the day we put our trust in Jesus, God himself moved in. The Spirit is a person living inside of us who helps, reminds, convicts, teaches, counsels, and leads us into all the ways of truth.[6]

That, my friends, is amazing!

What does God say to you when you listen to him?

Try it now. Seriously. Set down this book or your e-reader for five minutes and just be silent before God and listen. Don't speak to God — just listen.

[Five-minute pause]

Okay. What did you hear?

As I have been learning to quiet my mind and soul before God, most often the first thing I hear him say to me is, *I love you. You're my son, and I am delighted with you!* That blows me away. The creator God of the universe takes the time to speak to me, and the first thing out of his mouth is, *I love you.* God telling me I'm his loved son reminds me that I am part of his family and that there are many more runaway kids out there whom he loves and wants to bring home.

The reality that God the Father sent our Brother Jesus to come and show us his great love by giving up his life on a cross sends me out to tell others this good news. The words I hear the Spirit speak often point out ways I can serve others and show them this same love God has for them. He is still speaking.

What is God waiting to say to you?

THINGS TO THINK ABOUT

How often do you spend time earnestly listening to God?

Do you have a regular time where you experience listening to God through his Word?

What is the last thing you know for certain God spoke to you?

In what ways could you begin to cultivate the rhythm of *listening forward* to God through times of quiet and solitude?

How would the relationships in your life change if you spoke only what you heard God first speaking to you?

Chapter 9

EAT

Regularly eat meals with others as a way of inviting them into the family of God.

THE MUSIC WAS ON, a few candles were lit throughout the house, the pancake batter was mixed and ready to pour, and the coffee was brewing. "I think we're ready!" Tina hollered to me from the kitchen. It wasn't long before our home was once again filling up with friends from the neighborhood mixed with folks from my missional community.

"Breakfast Club" was officially in full swing!

We learned early on in Tacoma that one of the rhythms of our city was sleeping in late on Sunday mornings. After the rush of the work week, most people took it a lot slower on Sundays. The vast majority (more than 90 percent) would never choose to "go to church" on that day — or any day, for that matter — but they were open to stopping by to a sort of open-house breakfast/brunch thingy when it was convenient for them.

A steady flow of easy-to-make breakfast foods, strong coffee, and a few mimosas make for a very nonthreatening way to get into the rhythm of my neighbors. "Stopping in for a quick bite" seems to be much less intimidating than a sit-down dinner invitation. And for most everyone, after "risking" the first time at one of our breakfast feasts, they loved it and rarely missed one after that.

This not only became a rhythm in my neighborhood, but others in our church also started having impromptu breakfast clubs once a month or so. We only called them that among ourselves; we didn't advertise them as such with our neighbors. We just said, "Hey, stop on by anytime Sunday morning. We're having a breakfast/ brunch deal for the neighborhood between nine and noon. Hope you can make it!"

At one point, there were fifteen or sixteen of these little breakfast gatherings happening all over Tacoma on the same Sunday morning. Early on in our family history as Soma, we would take one Sunday a month, and instead of having our regular "service," or gathering together, we would send everyone out on mission in their own neighborhoods. These breakfast clubs served as a perfect way to engage people right where they lived — and it was always a big hit. Really. No special skills required to get into this rhythm.

The usual barriers of busyness, formality, and having a perfect space all melted away as we casually opened our homes to anyone interested. It was our way of saying to everyone, "Our door is always open to you; come on in!"

PULL UP A CHAIR

Eating meals with others not only shows care and inclusiveness, but the meals themselves embody love in community. They put flesh on the phrase "You're welcome here anytime." Meals turn outsiders into family.

Think about all that happens, and has happened, for you around the table. My wife and I both grew up in families that held the dinner hour as sacred. Regardless of what else was going on in life, in good times and in bad, and through less than perfect parenting, family dinner was where we all reached across the table to one another, sharing the victories and disappointments from our day.

As we began raising our own family, we made our dinner table a sacred space where we tried not to bring up discipline issues, bad grades, or gripes we had with one another; instead, we intentionally aimed at making it a time of encouragement. We wanted to truly value that time and always desire to be together for it. This imperfect family circle served as a reminder that we need one another and that God had given us to one another. These meals together reminded us that God is our provider and taught us the powerful significance of eating together.

A GLUTTON AND A DRUNKARD

Food and feasting have always played a prominent role throughout the Bible, serving as examples of and metaphors for what God is like, showing his great care and provision for those he loves. In fact, God's story starts out with the first humans, Adam and Eve, eating food that God had warned them not to eat, and it culminates with Jesus coming as the "bread of life" to meet humankind's greatest need.

There are three ways the New Testament completes the sentence, "The Son of Man came . . .": "The Son of Man [came not] to be served, but to serve, and to give his life as a ransom for many";[1] "The Son of Man came to seek and to save the lost";[2] and "The Son of Man came eating and drinking."[3] The first two are statements of purpose. Why did Jesus come? He came to serve, to give his life as a ransom, to seek and to save the lost. But the third is a statement of method. How did Jesus come? He came eating and drinking.[4]

Luke's gospel records at least nine different meals Jesus ate with people, and there are more throughout the New Testament. But Luke and the other authors are not just showing Jesus' humanity and talking about his human need to eat. They are communicating something much more profound regarding his mission.

The religious teachers in Jesus' day couldn't figure out what he was up to with all of his partying. Jesus, calling them on their assumptions, pointed out, "The Son of Man came eating and drinking, and you say, 'Here is a glutton and a drunkard, a friend of tax collectors and sinners.'"[5] In other words, Jesus' critics were accusing him of being a big fat drunk who hung out with sinners.

Ouch.

As one author put it, "This is why eating and drinking were so important in the mission of Jesus: they were a sign of his friendship with tax collectors and sinners. His 'excess' of food and 'excess' of grace are linked. In the ministry of Jesus, meals were enacted grace, community, and mission."[6] In Jesus' parable of the wedding banquet in Matthew 22, Jesus says in essence, "The kingdom of God is like a feast where the poor, broken, and outcast, the dirty and messed up, as well as my friends, all get invited in and seated next to me!"

> For Jesus ... "feast" was not just a "metaphor" for the kingdom. As Jesus announced the feast of the kingdom, He also brought it into reality through His own feasting. Unlike many theologians, He did not come preaching an ideology, promoting ideas, or teaching moral maxims. He came teaching about the feast of the kingdom, and He came feasting in the kingdom. Jesus did not go around merely talking about eating and drinking; He went around eating and drinking.[7]

Jesus ate with others — a lot! So should we.

LOVE FEST

If you've ever seen the movie *Babette's Feast*, then you know what a beautiful picture of God's grace a meal can be. In the film, Babette, a French refugee of war who had been a chef at a fine Parisian restaurant, shows up at the door of two stoic Christian sisters in nineteenth-century Denmark. After experiencing an unexpected financial gain, she implores the sisters to allow her to take charge of preparing a meal that is to be the center of a celebration honoring their dead father's one hundredth birthday. The sisters are secretly worried about what Babette, a Catholic and a French woman, might do, but they allow her to take charge of the meal after she insists on paying for everything herself. Babette then prepares the feast of a lifetime, costing her thousands of dollars — every last cent she has. The suspicious looks and awkward first tastes of luscious food and drink that the guests take at the beginning of the meal slowly turn to lavish joy and humble appreciation, a true picture of the kingdom feast Jesus talked about!

My wife is a lot like Babette. She loves to throw elaborate seven- and eight-course meals for our friends and neighbors several times each year. She calls them *love fests*. Tina is an amazing cook, and these dinner parties have become somewhat legendary in our circles. The meals take four to five hours to enjoy and are filled with succulence and surprise, laughter and grace. Our guests are always blown away by these extravagant offerings. Tina gives of herself completely, and she loves it!

One of these meals was given to honor a friend of ours, Brian, who was soon to be moving with his wife back to San Diego, where she was originally from. Brian was probably the most well-known and favorite bartender in our city. Everyone loved being around him, a crazy guy who had a magnetic personality, to say the least. When my son asked him if he was planning to throw a huge going-away party to accommodate all of his friends and admirers before leaving, he said to Lil' C, "You know what would be the best thing I could think of? It would be awesome if my wife and I could have dinner with you and your family. Do you think your folks would be up for something like that at your house?"

We were pretty blown away by this. Although we knew Brian from his bartending skills, we had not had that much meaningful contact with him. Or so we thought. Our son was a close friend with him, and he knew who I was and what we were about in our city, but his request came as a surprise.

"Of course we will!" we said. My wife was giddy as she planned one of her famous love fests. We would have eight courses that night with Brian, his wife, the five of us in our family, and three of his closest friends. Brian was expecting a normal, quiet dinner that evening with us and had absolutely no idea what was waiting for him.

Awesome, right?

As course after course rolled out, all perfectly paired with a nice juice or wine, Brian and his guests were a little shocked. What was going on? Appetizers, fruits, and cheeses arrived, then some soup, a salad, and two main courses. Then desserts and more cheeses.

"Why are you doing this for us?" they asked.

Brian's wife, Dana, started crying. She said that no one had ever done anything like that for her, or them, in their lives. We told them we loved them and felt honored to celebrate their lives and send them off with our best wishes — and we would miss them. "Now we don't want to move," they said. "We want to stay here with all of you guys!"

As I write this, tears flow from my eyes too. After Brian moved down to San Diego, things didn't work out as planned, and he ended up moving back six months later. Our relationship went to another level and our conversations were different, more trusting, more focused on eternal things — and Jesus. Brian had grown up going to church once in a while but never came to fully understand who Jesus was and what God really desired for his life. In our family, he found fellow travelers who accepted him and would answer his questions, who loved him right where he was at.

We were devastated when Brian unexpectedly died a few months later in a motorcycle accident. It seemed our entire city mourned that week. I know we did. It hit my son and daughter the hardest in our family. They were both with him that night minutes before the accident. We were heartbroken.

Brian's family, knowing of our affection for him, and how we had shown him such love and care, asked me to speak at his memorial when they scattered his ashes in the Puget Sound. I was able to tell them that in the grimmest of times, there is hope, that God loves us in such times, and that he had used Brian to show all of us his love too. I told them that on the day Brian left earth, he saw the face of Love and now knows truth in ways that we are yet to see as clearly. I went on to explain the gospel in simple, understandable terms. Brian's mother asked me afterward if I could give her a copy of what I had said because it had touched her so deeply.

A meal can be an open door into the kingdom.

WHAT'S FOR DINNER?

Although the elaborate, once-in-a-while feasts have some impact on people, inviting them into your regular routine, your "hallowed ground," as it were, of normal family life and its rhythms is even more effective. We have always had lots of young, unmarried people in it, and the single guys always seem to stop by around dinnertime. "Oh, um, yeah . . . I was just wondering what you guys were up to tonight, and I thought I would stop by and say hello." My wife always makes a place for them, and on many occasions we have been blown away when a guest at our table has said, "I have never done this before."

"What? Never had dinner?"

"No, sat down as a family and eaten a meal at the same time and talked about one another's day and life."

We have learned that the simplicity and yet the profundity of having a meal together has been lost for many in our culture today. But this gives us an awesome opportunity to share God's love and generosity with people while doing something we are already doing perhaps twenty-one times per week! All we have to do is invite someone to join us.

What would it be like if you were to invite just one or two not-yet believers to share a meal with you each week? You're eating anyway, so not much extra time is required. Do you think it could have an impact? I can assure you it will, for it presents a picture of the availability of the kingdom to all those who would enter in. Our family, our community, represents the open arms of God and a place at his dinner table.

While trying to get into a similar rhythm with our neighbors, we hosted a backyard barbecue every Friday evening for an entire summer. We went door to door and handed out simple flyers, inviting everyone who lived within the four square blocks surrounding our home. We knew that many would probably not make it, but at least we got to meet them and introduce ourselves, saying hi once a week. We usually provided the side dishes and drinks and asked people to bring whatever they wanted to put on the grill — and our missional community chipped in each week so we wouldn't go broke. This was a team effort, a way for our community to invite others to walk in the ways of Jesus with us together.

It didn't rain one single Friday that summer — a major miracle considering where we live and the normal weather patterns for the Pacific Northwest!

At first, three or four families joined us. My son and several of his friends who are also marines would usually show up. We had no great *evangelistic* goal, never a weird bait and switch; we just ate and talked and got to know one another. The weeks turned into months, and these Friday nights began to average between forty and fifty people. It was a blast. Most of our neighbors came and joined us at least once, and many of them made this a part of their own weekend rhythm.

One week my family went away on a vacation and forgot to tell everyone that we would not be able to host the cookout that week. Oops. The day we got back I ran into Mary, one of our neighbors, and it immediately dawned on me — *we forgot about Friday night!* I started to apologize to her, but she quickly stopped me.

"That's okay," she said. "We were all walking over here last Friday with our food and stuff, and when you weren't home, we just went over to Mike and Annie's house. We didn't need you." I was a little taken aback and disappointed at first, and I think she could read that on my face. "No, no, we missed you guys," she added, "but you have given us the neighborhood we've always dreamed of having!" After that, the Friday night barbecues started moving around the neighborhood to other homes, hosted by our new friends.

HANG LOOSE

Remember Shakabrah, that little neighborhood café I mentioned that we loved going to? It was our favorite place to get into the rhythm of eating with our friends and neighbors, but through a series of unfortunate events, the restaurant was going to close down.

What? we thought. *That can't happen; everyone loves this place!*

So along with our friends Jeff and Jayne, my wife and I bought Shakabrah. We hired all the staff back — including the former owner — and quickly learned just how much work it is to run a restaurant and café!

The staff and customers, many who eat there seven days a week, have now become part of our extended family. We love them dearly, and I could tell many stories of how this place has become an extension of our own home. It is another little *table of grace* in our city that serves breakfast all day.

Not everyone will have the opportunity, desire, or skills to operate a café or restaurant. You don't need to. You have endless opportunities to eat with others, in the rhythm of your own life, as an invitation into the family of God.

BUT SOMETIMES IT'S HARD ...

Along the way, as I've shared these stories with others who desire to live as a blessing in their community, I have heard some of these refrains repeatedly:

> "I've got three kids and a house to keep clean on top of all the other chores and running around I have to do. How would I ever have people over for meals on a regular basis?"
> "I'm not that good of a cook, so I would not be able to put on elaborate meals — all fancy and everything. Besides, our house is too small for that kind of stuff."
> "There is no way we could afford to have people over so often. Our current family budget is maxed already!"

This list certainly isn't exhaustive, but maybe one or more of these refrains hit you where you're at. Here's a list of a few things we've had to learn to die to in order to open up our homes and mealtimes to others on a consistent basis:

A perfectly clean home
Perfectly behaved kids
Home furnishings that look straight out of a magazine
People touring the rooms of our home and seeing all the
stuff we hid away for a reason

Cooking skills on par with Martha Stewart
A great attitude at all times

I want to assure you that it is not your perfect home or your award-winning cooking skills that people are dying for. Letting go of these expectations requires me to believe, in the moment, that this is not really all about me; it is about Jesus being seen and experienced through us. Our neighbors don't need an amazing meal; they need us to be Jesus with flesh on. True hospitality is about having an attitude and posture that says to others, "You are always invited to join us; whatever we're eating, you are welcome."

Now you might be thinking, *I am not one of those people. I could never do all this and be the life of the party.* I want to point out here that you only need one or two people with crazy, outgoing social skills in your entire community — but you'll need many others who will be good friends, listeners, and encouragers. I've already said this, but it bears repeating — life on mission with God is something to be done in community. We really need one another. When we bring our differences *and* our favorite dish to share, our broken pasts *along with* a great dessert, we are indeed a picture of God's kingdom.

COMMON UNION

For me, the greatest picture of life in the kingdom is expressed every time a few of us share in the Lord's Supper together. This is probably the most famous meal Jesus ever had. It is unquestionably the most significant. Sharing simple communion (common union) together magnifies what we hope to experience, as Jesus did, with others at every meal we have. Jesus' last meal with his disciples before going to the cross was a new kingdom rhythm for all of us.

So next time you're all together, take out some bread and a cup of something delicious to drink. Examine your hearts in prayer, and then look into the eyes of those around you. Invite everyone to say yes to our King with whatever faith they have today. As the bread is passed around, little pieces being torn from the lump, and sips being taken from the cup, be reminded of something eternally profound: we are all in need, we are all hungry, and only God can provide what is necessary to fill our stomachs and satisfy our greatest hunger in life — himself.

There is a new kingdom, and its King has come.

THINGS TO THINK ABOUT

How often do you have others over to your home for a meal? Do you invite both believers and not-yet believers? How often are you invited to a meal by a non-Christian?

When you think about beginning to live in a rhythm of eating with others, what challenges do you see? What fears arise in your heart?

How would living together in community help eliminate any barriers to this rhythm?

Who are three people or couples you could invite over for a meal in the very near future?

Chapter 10

BLESS

Regularly bless others through words, actions, or gifts.

BOB IS A TALL, outspoken Italian stallion of a guy who lives life as large as anybody I've ever known. Not long after I met my buddy Bob, he took me golfing at one of the nicest golf clubs in our state — much nicer than I am used to. I'm more like a landscaper digging holes than a golfer. A month or so later, Bob took me fly-fishing up in the beautiful Wenatchee Valley. I am also no good at fly-fishing, but we had a great time enjoying each other and the breathtaking surroundings up there in the river valley. Then we tried salmon fishing from Bob's boat on the Puget Sound.

After a while Bob said, "I hope you don't mind, but I took the liberty of packing this here cooler up with a bunch of ice-cold drinks, and I threw in some fried chicken in case you get hungry."

I hope you don't mind? What?

He was joking of course, but it revealed his heart to me, for he lives to be a blessing to others. He doesn't have to work all that hard at it because it has become the rhythm of his life. Bob lives to make sure others (including me) are blessed, rested, and restored.

Bob is not a rich man, by the way; he has spent his life working among the homeless and addicted in our city, but he feels very blessed by God in his life, and he lives to pass on that blessing.

Blessed to be a blessing.

This rhythm of blessing flows directly out of our servant identity. It is who Jesus was when he was on earth, and it is who we now are.

A "DEALING WITH MY STUFF" PROBLEM

What if you were to make a list of everything you have in life. I mean *everything*. We all came into the world with nothing, so everything we now have has ultimately been given to us by God: homes, cars, toys, tools, clothing, friends, education, talents, experiences, parents, upbringing, furniture, dishes — how big and long would this list be? Some friends of mine who live as a missional community decided to take out some of those big, wall-sized sticky notes one evening and actually list everything they could think of — everything they had individually and collectively. The list was overwhelming as page after page filled the walls. There were hundreds of things on that list.

Then they stopped and asked themselves a question: *Why do we have all of these things? Why has God given all of this to us? Is it for us to hoard and enjoy for ourselves alone?*

Scripture provides the answer to those questions:

God is able to bless you abundantly, so that in all things at all times, having all that you need, you will abound in every good work. As it is written:

"They have freely scattered their gifts to the poor;
their righteousness endures forever."

... This service that you perform is not only supplying the

needs of the Lord's people but is also overflowing in many expressions of thanks to God.[1]

God has given us all things that we would be blessed, bless others, and show his glory. When we bless others, we are doing two things. First, we are passing on God's rich harvest — paying it forward, if you will. Second, we are showing our thankfulness to God for blessing us in the first place. The Bible teaches that to live our lives as a blessing to others is actually to live a life of thankfulness.

A DOUBLE GLOVER

Earlier I told you about my neighbor Hal, the old guy from my neighborhood with the oxygen bottle and the WWII uniform. One day his wife, Gail, came knocking on my door and said, "I am going to California to visit my sister for three weeks, and I was wondering if you would mind looking in on Hal for me once in a while until I get back." I assured her that I was happy to do that; in fact, I would look forward to it.

On one of my rounds, stopping in to see Hal, I stood knocking on his door for longer than usual. His car was out front, so I knew he was home. I started wondering if he was all right. He finally answered the door in his pajamas (in the middle of the afternoon), and a look of pain was etched across his face.

"What's up, Hal?" I asked. "Is everything all right?"

"Come in, come in," he said. "I have to go back upstairs to my room and lie down. My feet are killing me." I looked down at his bare feet and couldn't help notice that they were *extremely* swollen, red, and sort of breaking open with something that resembled motor oil oozing out. No wonder they hurt!

I followed Hal up to his room. I had never been up there before. He flopped down onto his twin-sized bed with a grimace and propped his feet up on a pillow. I asked him what was wrong; I had never noticed him having such problems before. He always seemed to get around pretty well for such an old buck.

He told me that he had a condition that caused the swelling and that usually Gail was home to put a special ointment on his feet that helped the problem. But she was in California, and he was unable to reach down and apply the salve himself. "She usually puts on that medicine right there," he said, "over on the dresser." He pointed to a huge tube with a red cap and a pharmacy label on it.

Gulp.

I looked down at his scaly, swollen feet only eighteen inches away from my face, and then I looked back at the tube on his dresser. "Um, this right over here?"

"Yep, that's the magical stuff."

Well, you can imagine what was racing through my mind. The Holy Spirit let me know what I had to do — no, *got* to do. "Would it be okay, Hal, if I put some of that on your feet for you?"

"Yes, that would be great."

I felt like I wanted to run out and put on one of those yellow hazmat suits for handling hazardous materials — this was a real "double glover"! But I proceeded to butter up his feet with the ointment, and for the next several days, I continued helping my friend Hal care for his feet until Gail got home.

I thought about this experience a lot. In that moment, everything in me wanted to say something such as, "I'll pray for your feet, Hal" — and then run home and hope someone else would show up to help him. I decided that having to deal with the infected feet of a friend was nothing compared to how Jesus had served this sick and infected guy from Tacoma — even to the point of having nails pounded through *his* feet to do so. We bless because we have been so radically and thoroughly blessed and served by Jesus with his entire life. It's not that we have to or *should* serve others; we bless others out of our gratefulness.

A RHYTHM OF BLESSING

Stop and picture something with me for a moment. What if you were part of a group of friends who all lived near one another or worked at the same place, and you all started blessing at least three people each week? You lived in a rhythm of blessing, asking God, "Who do you want to show your love and care to today?" What would that say about your identity and who God is to those around you? Do you think people would notice if you lived in this rhythm? Do you think they would begin to wonder, *What is up with you? Why are you people this way?*

They will, and they do. When we live to bless others, the explanations for our faith and what we believe to be true about Jesus do not fall on deaf ears.

To get into this rhythm, I have found it helps to think and pray about blessing others in three different ways: through words, actions, and gifts. Let me run through a few of my favorite memories to give you some examples of what this can look like.

WORD BLESSINGS

As I mentioned earlier, I love pointing out to someone how they've displayed some characteristic of God, or how something they did reminds me of Jesus. This is especially surprising for those who are not yet believers!

I once told a friend who is an atheist that the knowledge and wisdom with which he conducted his business was remarkable. I said that I believed that all wisdom comes from God, and then I added, "I think you have God-given wisdom, and it reminds me of what

God is like." I thought he was going to fall over. It changed him a little, and it changed our relationship.

Another time, I told a neighbor that the way she laid down some of her preferences so that she could bless one of my daughters in a particular situation reminded me of the way Jesus laid down his life. She was blown away. "I'll have to think about that," she said, trailing off.

I have received countless little notes and cards in which people have taken a few moments to thank me for something or tell me how God used me in their lives. They are small things that didn't cost them much in time or money, but I am always superblessed by these words, which often came at a time when it felt like someone was throwing me a life preserver.

It's easy to pick up the phone and thank someone for how they served or blessed you, or just to tell them how much you love them. "I was thinking of all the blessings God has poured into my life, and I thought of you. I just wanted you to know that."

At times I will pray and ask God, "Who do you want me to bless today?" He always answers that question — usually quickly and clearly. Usually it's something like, "I want you to call Aaron and tell him how thankful you are for his gift of music." Or "Point out to Sarah how blessed everyone was when she showed up to the party the other night with that huge shrimp platter. So generous!"

ACTION BLESSINGS

Action blessings can run the gamut from something small that someone can do on their own to community-size blessings that take more time and effort as a group.

I'm away a lot traveling, and so my wife feels extremely loved and cared for when someone gives her a call or stops by to make sure she and my daughters are doing okay. We have had brothers and sisters in the community come over at the drop of a hat just to check on a suspicious noise outside, repair a leaky toilet, kill a giant spider, or drop off meals. It doesn't have to be anything very elaborate; it's still a blessing for sure.

My friends Hannah and Todd have three kids and also live a pretty active life. Their community has been growing and learning to be a blessing in some pretty cool ways. Hannah first met her neighbor Jackie out in front of the house while playing with the kids one day. Jackie was going through a messy divorce and was really in need of some friends. Over time they grew closer as they walked their kids around the neighborhood, visited the zoo, and did a lot of normal "mom stuff" together. One day, several months ago, Hannah asked Jackie what she was doing that day. "I am heading up to my grandmother's house to do my laundry," she replied. "It's over an hour away, but at least it's free!"

In that moment, the Spirit made it clear what he wanted Hannah to do. Jackie lived only a few blocks away, and Hannah figured that her washing machine just sat there much of the week, so why not start blessing Jackie? For over six months, Hannah did laundry for Jackie and the kids every week. Jackie dropped it off in the morning on the way to work, and on her way home in the evening, she picked it up all clean and folded.

"Jackie thought I was crazy," Hannah told me. "She wouldn't believe me when I told her that it was fun turning her dirty laundry into clean laundry." Hannah cherished the chance to talk with Jackie during these drop-off and pick-up times. "Each time she gets a little taste of Jesus," she said, "and what he is like."

Months went by as Hannah and Todd, along with their missional community, blessed Jackie and her kids, treating them as part of their family. She had many questions about God and Jesus and her faith. All that laundry time was paying off! Recently Jackie committed her life to Jesus, stepping from darkness into light — and with clean clothes on! Is doing someone else's laundry a big thing or a little thing? You can decide, but it certainly made an eternal difference in Jackie's life.

Here's an example that combines gifts with actions and took our entire community to pull together. Lakisha was in a world of hurt when Diane met her. She had a job, but as a single mom with several kids, she had fallen horribly far behind on her bills. Even after using up all of the state aid she qualified for, she was just days away from having her electricity turned off. To keep the power on, Lakisha needed to pay $1,700 by the weekend. There was no way she could come up with that kind of money. Diane, who works as a nurse, raised all the money she could from people in her missional community and then asked people in our other communities if they could help. Together, *our* family was able to pay that bill, blessing Lakisha and *her* family.

My wife and some of the other sisters then helped Lakisha set up a budget and organize her huge pile of bills and late notices. They took her shopping and showed her how to save money on groceries. They even helped her repair her credit rating so she could qualify for a car loan. She had been spending hundreds of dollars each month in taxi rides that she could not afford, but she needed to get to work. We gave her a computer to help manage her finances and taught her how to set up and use the software. All of this took months and was as much a blessing to us as it was to her. That's how it seems to work; when we obediently and joyfully serve others with the same spirit that Christ served us, we feel blessed too.

We ran into Lakisha several months later, and she told us that she had been able to pay off her bills in full. She had even managed to put away $1,500 in savings and was very thankful for our help. "I have always lived hand to mouth month to month," she said, "so to now have my bills paid, a car that runs, and money in the bank is a miracle. Praise Jesus!"

Lakisha was never a "formal member" of our church. She never joined our missional community, but she was a part of our family because God brought her to us and called us to bless her with the abundance he had given us. In God's economy we don't give to get; we give because we've already been given so much.

GIFT BLESSINGS

Remember my friend Bob from earlier in this chapter? One day we were walking together on our way to lunch in a somewhat sketchy part of town (where he likes to hang out), and an old, unwashed beggar came up to us and asked for any spare change we might be able to give him.

"What do you want this money for?" Bob asked him. Amazingly, the guy actually admitted to us that he wanted the money to go buy some beer. Bob reached into his pocket and pulled out the change that he found. Fifty cents. Holding the money out in the palm of his hand, he told the man, "Someone in your life has been telling you that you need to stop all of this and that they love you and want to help you. I want to encourage you to listen to that person. Now, I am going to give you this fifty cents. This is God's money, not mine. You do whatever you think God would have you do with it. I hope you have a great day, brother!"

Later, as Bob and I were out for lunch, he bought meals for three people in the restaurant who were in the military — just to bless them. They never knew who paid for their lunch.

Bob is crazy generous with the blessings!

Finally, here is my personal favorite blessing story. It combines all three types of blessings, and *I* was the recipient!

Recently I turned fifty years old. I didn't really want a party, but my wife and daughters insisted they do *something*. Just as we were starting a small and intimate dinner celebration, someone grabbed me in a huge bear hug from behind. It was my son, Caesar, who is a marine stationed in San Diego. He had flown in to surprise me for my birthday! We had a great night together, and having all my kids, Tina, and my closest friends with me was wonderful. During the dinner, my son handed me an envelope and told me, "Read this later when you have some time. I love you, Pops!"

So after a few more stops that evening, including another larger surprise from friends who gathered at our café (not what I asked for, *honey*), I went home for the night feeling loved, thankful, and tired. I remembered the envelope from my son and retrieved it from my jacket pocket. Inside was a letter he had written to me. In it were all the words a father could ever hope to hear from his son. It was gracious and full of praise, and it expressed his love and respect for me. He also commented that he was now the same age I was when he was born, and that he could not imagine the kind of sacrifices he would have to make if he were a father right now. He went on to say, "You made those kinds of sacrifices for me, Pops. One of those sacrifices was when you sold your Harley to finance family and life stuff. But you also gave me a love for riding, and it doesn't seem right that you don't have a motorcycle to ride."

There was one more thing in that envelope — the title to a Harley-Davidson. My son *gave me* a motorcycle for my birthday! I could hardly believe it. Who does that sort of thing?

Talk about being blessed! I was.

I am.

One of my absolute favorite things now is to go riding with my son. It's hard to explain, but sometimes blessings come in chromed steel and are really loud as they fly down the road!

BUT SOMETIMES IT'S HARD ...

There have been times in our community when the needs of others seem to go on and on. Often even after we have helped someone, they ask for more. We can start to think that if we keep blessing them they will start — or maybe already are — taking advantage of us. I have heard people say, "They got themselves into this; if they made better choices, they wouldn't be in such a mess! I don't think we should help them anymore."

Yeah, I get it — just like you and me in practically every area of our lives.

That's why we need a savior. That's why God sent his one and only Son to lay down his life, to rescue us from all of that sinful junk, including our selfish choices and lack of belief in our Daddy's great generosity.

We were born naked, with nothing, and that is how we will leave this world. I see it this way: my stuff is your stuff, because ultimately it is not our stuff. As God's family, we treat our earthly possessions as blessings that we have been given to be a blessing to others.

It's all God's stuff.

The definition of discipleship I gave earlier is the process of moving from unbelief to belief about who God is and what he has done in absolutely every area of life. The reason we often are not generous is because we have not yet been "saved" in this area of our lives. We do not fully believe we have a generous God who can meet all our needs and the needs he brings to our attention.

He can.

There might be a reason you noticed that child who comes home to an empty house after school every day. Maybe the single mom you met recently who is struggling to pay her bills or buy Christmas presents for her kids is not just someone random.

Have you ever stopped to think, *God pretty much only uses* people *to bless other people?* Rarely does a meal or a pile of money ever just show up. God uses his family to provide these things.

It is our heritage, our identity, and our birthright to live as a blessing on God's behalf.

A CONDUIT OR A BARREL?

A conduit is like a pipe. It is something that water, electricity, or any other supply is routed through to another place. A barrel is for storing up resources — for holding on to them for later use.

God is looking for conduits of his grace and generosity. He is not looking for barrels to store these things in. Coveting our things and acting as if we are our own source of income, supply, money, time, and so on shows that our hearts are not at peace and ultimately trusting God for these things. We hang on to our stuff because we believe it is in short supply.

Which do you most often represent, a conduit or a barrel?

Whenever my wife, Tina, and I have prayed about giving a certain amount of money to someone or some need, we have usually either ended up with the exact same number in mind or Tina has come up with a number much bigger than mine. But she has never once thought about giving less than I was prepared to give. Her heart of generosity has helped remind me over and over again that she sees God as a great and generous God, able to refill the barrel if we will but trust him and pour it out for others.

Go ahead and tip over that barrel!

PASS IT ON

You see, we don't go around preaching about ourselves. We preach that Jesus Christ is Lord, and we ourselves are your servants for Jesus' sake. For God, who said, "Let there be light in the darkness," has made this light shine in our hearts so we could know the glory of God that is seen in the face of Jesus Christ.

We now have this light shining in our hearts, but we ourselves are like fragile clay jars containing this great treasure. This makes it clear that our great power is from God, not from ourselves.[2]

The world is watching and our neighbors and coworkers are paying attention, so let's pour out more of God's blessings into their lives and see if he doesn't turn up the faucet of his grace. Every blessing we've received from God is like a sacred trust that will be continued only as we use it to show others his love.

Our salvation is not ours alone; it also belongs to every person on the face of the earth who hasn't had the opportunity of hearing the Good News and being restored to the Father through Jesus. Our faith and maturity have been given to us so that others may grow and walk in the light that we now reflect. Our costly healing belongs to some fellow sufferer that they too may find hope and be cured. Every experience of ours has also been shaped for another heart and will enable us to meet great needs if we are attentive to the opportunities God gives.[3]

As we've received, let us pass it on. We have truly been blessed to be a blessing.

THINGS TO THINK ABOUT

When you notice that something is broken or messy in life, do you look for ways to help or are you quicker to complain or secretly wish someone else would deal with it?

Do you feel like God has blessed you in your life? In what ways?

What has God given you in life that he may be waiting to use to bless others with and show his love uniquely through you?

Who are three people you could bless this week in word, action, or gift?

Chapter 11

CELEBRATE

*Regularly gather to celebrate and display
God's extravagant blessings.*

AS YOU CAN PROBABLY TELL by now, we like to throw neighborhood parties, going door-to-door beforehand handing out invitations. Toward the beginning of one of these evening parties, seven or eight people had drifted in and out when the doorbell rang again. It was a couple we had never met before, Ryan and Liz, both doctors. They had bought a house around the corner from us, the cute three-tone green one, but had not moved in yet.

"We got this invitation to your party," they said. "We can't stay tonight, but we at least wanted to meet you and say how cool it is to see a neighborhood where people actually know each other and hang out. We're so excited to be moving in next month!" Off they went, back into the dark, our entire conversation lasting maybe ten minutes.

A few months later, after a couple more times of getting to hang out together, Liz told me, "Ryan and I don't go to church or anything, but when we have kids we are going to take them to your church." I had never mentioned I was a pastor or anything about Soma. So I asked, "Why is that?"

"Because we want them to grow up serving people and loving their neighbors the way you all do."

Now we had not really been around them that much, to be truthful. We had treated them like our family in small ways, but the open door and casual acceptance they felt from our community had spoken volumes to their hearts already.

That is precisely the point of our celebrations — that people would both see the heart of our God and feel invited to the party.

A PARTY PEOPLE

Wouldn't it be great to overhear someone at a café in your town saying, "I don't know if I believe what those Christians believe, but they sure know how to throw a party!" That should be happening — all the time. The church I am a part of has been called "the party church." Awesome! The church — God's body of believers — should be the most celebratory people on the planet! Just think about all that we have to celebrate.

We are forgiven for all of our sins, even the ones we have not committed yet.

We have been transformed into a new creation, and have new God-given identities.

We represent God as his missionary family everywhere we go as he now lives in us.

Oh, yeah — and we get to *live forever*!

That is something to celebrate, don't you think? We should be throwing parties and participating in celebrations — big and small — all the time.

A REMINDER AND A DEMONSTRATION

God called Israel to live in a rhythm of celebration. He mandated for them a series of annual festivals and feasts to be held every year without fail. All these celebrations served as reminders of God's goodness (all foreshadowing Jesus' life and death) and how the people were actually to live in light of this *every* day — not just during the festivals.

"Oh, is it that season already, time for the feast of firstfruits? God really has provided in abundance again this year!" Month after month, season after season, Israel's national celebrations served as a reminder of God's generosity, protection, and presence, while also serving as a demonstration to other nations of what their God was like. Who he was. That he alone was worthy to throw parties for. All the time.

As we saw earlier, Jesus was the same way. He was regularly eating and celebrating with people — so much so, in fact, that he had a reputation for it. I love that Jesus' first miracle was at a party. He was at a wedding with a bunch of wealthy people, and they are three days into the party when the wine ran out. Jesus took huge jugs of water and turned them into hundreds of gallons of the best wine the guests had ever tasted. By doing so, he was revealing something about his Father and the kingdom that day.

Jesus wants us to see that any picture of God we hold, any understanding of his Father we embrace that does not have at its core — as our central understanding — a celebration in which God is the provider, caregiver, and protector is twisted. He reminded us of this with his life, and he wants us to live as a demonstration of this truth to everyone.

How are we doing at celebrating to the glory of God?

A CELEBRATION OF GRACE

Graduating from high school and receiving my diploma was a big deal. My parents threw me a huge party, friends and relatives from all over (some I didn't even know) showed up with well wishes, congratulations, and those all-important cards with money tucked

164

into them! People came out of the woodwork to support and encourage me.

When Kirstan, who I shared about earlier, graduated and received her high school GED, she was not expecting anything like that to happen for her. She had never seen or experienced such a thing. But her friends and family in the missional community had other plans. When they asked her what she thought of the idea, however, at first she was hesitant. "I've never had a party. We never celebrate in my family. Getting together on the holidays was when everyone got mean and drunk. There was a lot of screaming and fighting."

This was going to be different.

The group sent out fancy invitations to everyone they could think of, asking them to come and help mark this milestone in her life. Finally, the day of the party arrived, though Kirstan wasn't expecting much. When she walked into the house, however, there was a massive number of balloons, a special cake, a barbecue grill filled with burgers out back, desserts, and around forty or fifty people — all there for her! Her extended family, neighbors, friends, everyone from her missional community, and people from other missional communities in Soma attended the party.

And many brought gifts and cards with money. (I still love that part best.)

Network Tacoma, who still provided the apartment she and her mom lived in, had recently received a donated car that was in great shape, so they gave her that as a graduation present. Her first car! Kirstan was pretty much blown away by all of this. She shared with her missional community, "I think I am getting grace, understanding what it's all about."

My wife, Tina, and I were there that day too. There was a wonderful sense of triumph and joy and grace. Our hearts were full.

Everyone was there to celebrate our sister Kirstan, but we were there to celebrate Jesus too. What I mean is that we have all experienced failures, stops and starts, and times when second chances were needed in our lives. Jesus was patient with us. He was there for us, paved the way, and cheered us on. When we celebrate with one another, we are ultimately acknowledging God's greatest provision and "Hooray!" ever.

Jesus.

His perfect life reflected his trust in his Father's provision and showed us what it's like to live life to the fullest, close to God, showing the world that we have something amazing to celebrate!

MY HEAD HURTS

As a community, we have thrown parties for every imaginable reason, just to be with one another regularly. I've already shared with you about our weekly Friday night barbecues. Awesome. For several years, my wife and I hosted New Year's Day parties. A lot of people in our neighborhood and throughout the city go out for some heavy partying on New Year's Eve, and they all have one thing in common the next day. They are *hungry* — and maybe a little hungover. We don't usually get things started until around noon, when everyone wakes up, and then we just serve a ton of comfort food and a *lot* of coffee. This has given us one more unique way to serve our friends and get into their rhythms, even if we didn't stay out all night.

People are always celebrating something. There are endless things being celebrated that we can participate in: birthday parties, graduations, Christmas, New Year, Halloween, Super Bowl Sunday, a promotion or raise at work — you get the picture. Not only can we throw great celebrations as a demonstration of God's heart, but we can also join in the celebrations of others and be the "bringers of the better wine," as Jesus was. Maybe for you it's not wine, but it might be a humongous platter of shrimp!

MR. CLARK

My family and I live right next door to a Salvation Army food bank, and there is always a steady stream of "mission opportunities" standing in line each day. Over the years, we have gotten to know many of the staff and volunteers that serve there. One day I heard my doorbell ring and could see a shadow cast across my front porch. I am not sure why, or how I knew it, but sure enough, it was Mr. Clark.

"Hello, Reverend!" he said. (He always called me that.) "D'ya mind if I come in for a minute? I have somethin' to ask you."

Mr. Clark had become my friend over the years as we sat out front under the shade of one of my trees and talked. He liked to smoke his ever-present pipe, and at times I would join him. He was around seventy-five or eighty years old and wore a suit and tie *every* day, which only added to his regal look. Mr. Clark had come over to tell me he was getting married, and he wanted to know if I would perform their ceremony. The woman he was to wed was in her midforties (nice job, Mr. Clark!) and had been caring for him for a while, and he wanted to marry her before he got "too old." Not long after that, we all got together to discuss their relationship and how God sees marriage, and to plan the wedding.

I performed the simple ceremony late in the morning one sunny day on my back deck. My wife and daughters were the only ones present besides the bride and groom. Tina made fried chicken with all the fixin's for lunch. We had a local bakery make them a cake, and we went through all of the small rituals that made this a special day. I have lots of photos from that morning. What a hoot! My daughter Christin loved getting to sign the official wedding certificate as one of the witnesses.

I remember thinking how odd yet awesome it was that I had met Mr. Clark and now got to share in celebrating the next chapter in his long and interesting story. I can't imagine I will ever experience a wedding celebration quite like it again. Thanks, God!

When two people choose to lay down their lives for each other, submitting their plans and hopes to the Father, it is a powerful picture of the life of Jesus — a beautiful display of the gospel. So weddings are a big deal in our community. These celebrations become markers of God's grace throughout our combined journey, and they are some of our favorite memories together. "Isn't that the minister out there doing the Worm on the dance floor?"

"Yes, in fact, I do believe that is the pastor who spoke earlier . . . and he's pretty good at that!"

FAMILY REUNION

I have had many people tell me, "This thing feels like a big celebration, kind of like a family reunion!" after joining the Soma family at one of our Sunday gatherings in Tacoma. Once a week we have a combined get-together of our missional communities, something that resembles a "church service" that we call our *family gathering*. These times are filled with the gospel being proclaimed, food, laughter, music, and sometimes a little dancing in the back. We have one young man who has always liked to twirl around in the back with his arms raised during the music. Pretty cool.

It's a time that feels much like a weekly family reunion where everyone is coming together to celebrate all that God has done in and through our lives that week together on his mission. We also invite others to the party so they will see and hear and taste how awesome our heavenly Dad and his Son are! At times on one of our Sunday gatherings, instead of preaching and singing and our normal revelry, we have an old-fashioned potluck feast together. We call these agape feasts, and we take two or three hours to be together and celebrate God's generosity through a cornucopia of amazing foods that remind us of how creative and giving our Father God is.

We tend to want to do these types of parties and celebrations as an "event" rather than in rhythm. "Remember when we threw that awesome party for the neighbors last year on the Fourth of July?" But celebration needs to be a rhythm in our lives the same as our weekly Friday night barbecues or the way we gather on Sundays. Celebrating as a rhythm of life is not just about going to or throwing lots of parties; sometimes it's a bunch of us going to the awards ceremony for one of the kids in our community when he receives an award at school. Or going to watch the daughters of a couple in the neighborhood perform in their school Christmas pageant. Maybe several of us will go to watch the soccer game of one of the boys in our missional community and cheer our heads off.

"Who are all your fans, Justin?"

"Oh, they're friends of mine. Part of my family . . . I mean, my church. We do lots of stuff together."

BUT SOMETIMES IT'S HARD ...

We know that when God made the world and everything in it, he pronounced it all "very good." Everything in life is meant to bring glory to God, showing some aspect of his character and love. Sin is a perversion of things God originally created good but that became distorted or twisted to glorify or serve something or someone other than God.

When a man and a woman enjoy sex in marriage, it is a good thing. Actually it is a great thing! But pornography or rape is a sinful distortion of what God created for our good. All the variety of flavors, texture, and colors that we can experience with food are a gift from God. Food sustains and nourishes us. But overeating to the point of obesity or addiction is sinful.

In everything, we need to ask, Who gets the glory? Who is this serving? The apostle Paul said, "If I take part in the meal with thankfulness, why am I denounced because of something I thank God for? So whether you eat or drink or whatever you do, do it all for the glory of God."[1]

The same principle holds true for celebration. Are we celebrating in ways that demonstrate the love and redemption Christ offers? Are we helping others see what a "redeemed" party or partier looks like? Paul exhorted the Corinthians, "Be on your guard; stand firm in the faith; be courageous; be strong. Do everything in love."[2]

Our goal as we celebrate is for people to see and know God and grow in their trust of him, just as all of the celebrations God gave Israel pointed to the redemptive work of Jesus. Faith, love, and redemption should motivate *all* of our celebrations.

BOTTOMS UP?

So what do we do with the issue of drinking alcohol? There are three commonly held views. Some hold to a strong prohibitionist perspective and believe the Bible teaches that alcohol consumption is strictly forbidden. Others think that although the Bible does not expressly forbid the drinking of alcoholic beverages, drinking in our society is often reckless and should not be condoned; therefore, Christians should abstain from participating. Many others have the opinion that alcohol is permitted for Christians as long as it's consumed in moderation and in a careful manner.

So which is the right perspective?

Followers of Jesus need to inhabit our cities and so inhabit our neighborhoods and pubs and clubs that those who are not yet following Jesus would know what it looks like to live as a Christian who goes to a pub. Christ seekers watching us may be wondering, *What would it look like if I were to be a Christian and celebrate the big things of life, or for that matter, the small things of life? What would my alcohol drinking look like, and what should my attitude be?*

Our lives should be their answer and their example — a picture of redemption. If our lives have been redeemed, then our response to cultural abuses is not to abstain but to redeem. That not only pushes us to maturity by teaching us how to eat or drink to the glory of God; it is also a witness to the world that God can and does redeem.

If we abstain or retract from culture as our response to sin in the world, we miss embodying and expressing redemption, and I'm afraid the message we will send is that what God created good can be perverted beyond redemption — that the gospel is not big enough to redeem this part of life and culture. And if not this, then maybe it is not big enough to deal with the rest of my sin either: my marriage, my addiction, my fear. *Me.*

And one of the most awesome things about being part of God's family is that we get to engage the world as a part of his plan for redemption.

BUCKLE UP!

Both abusive self-focus and religion have given celebration a black eye. Many people see being a Christian as the death of a life that includes anything fun. Christians often abstain from *everything* because they don't want to get any sin on them or be associated with "that type of people." It's time we show this world that a life lived indwelt by the Spirit of God, a life of perfect acceptance, knowing that our King comes back victorious in the end, is an exhilarating thrill ride and the most amazing adventure we could ever hope for.

I need the constant reminder of God's goodness that living in a rhythm of celebration gives. My city needs the demonstration that God has a family that believes he is a good and generous Father who loves to party and is not afraid to bring the wine. Life lived with joy, expressing what we believe to be true about us — because it is true of God — is our greatest act of worship. The world needs to see more of this.

We are the celebration! Our lives are a megawatt bulb of proof that Jesus is truly King, and his kingdom is great. Ultimately, celebration is not something we do, it is something we embody. It is a state of the soul. A heart thing. We can be sitting at a large, loud party with lights spinning, glitzy drink fountains splashing, and people dancing all around us, yet our hearts can be far from celebratory. Likewise, we can be sitting alone on a beach, at a desk, or on our couch, and things may not be going perfectly in our day, but our heart, our soul, can be rejoicing and celebrating our great inheritance in Christ.

I long for our neighborhoods to be filled with pockets of God's people who raise a glass of invitation to all fellow strugglers on the journey, letting everyone know that it is going to be all right, that there is hope and help. That they won't have to go this life alone. King Jesus is alive and coming back, and until then we have one another. And when he comes, he has promised to drink a glass of wine with all of us.[3]

I cannot wait for that day.

THINGS TO THINK ABOUT

What are your favorite types of celebrations? What do you celebrate the most?

How are those celebrations a reminder of the gospel?

How could celebrations be infused with good news that serves as a demonstration of what Jesus is truly like? Who should participate in these celebrations?

How would others in your city respond to a family of missionaries who partied like crazy to God's glory?

When's your next celebration?

Chapter 12

RE-CREATE

*Take time to rest, play, create, and restore
beauty in ways that reflect God to others.*

I HAVE A LOVE-HATE RELATIONSHIP with my garden and
flower beds. On one hand, I love when they are clean, planted,
and blooming at all the right times each season. On the other,
because of the rains that are present throughout every season
in Tacoma, I have a nonstop battle with weeds that remain the
fastest-growing and most robust plants I have. They even flourish
during the winter when everything else is either dead or taking a
break.

I was working on the garden in front of my house one sunny afternoon (yes, we do get sun in the Pacific Northwest too!), and as
I pulled weeds and replaced them with bright, colorful flowers,
something started to shift in me. My heart softened as my nails
became caked with rich, black soil. I started feeling as if I was
involved in a much grander project or purpose, as if I was con-
necting to the overarching restoration of all things that God has
promised to do in our world.

Is my front garden a part of that? In that moment, it sure seemed
like it. The Spirit reminded me that this is how he works within me

too, pulling one weed at a time and replacing it with something beautiful. I started to think of all the people I know with weeds and thorny, spiky parts of their personalities and lives. Maybe I was to be patient and willing to get my hands a little dirty helping to "beautify the garden" of their lives too.

One by one, people from the neighborhood started to notice what I was up to. "Wow! That is looking really beautiful. I just *love* petunias!" "I was wondering if you were ever going to get around to this project." (Not the feedback I hoped for, but I'll take it.) One of the workers from the Salvation Army next door who loves to give me gardening advice ambled over and said, "This is looking really good. I think I'll start taking my breaks over here in front of your house from now on." My flower beds were becoming his own little garden of Eden in the neighborhood. A simple hour or two of gardening had refreshed and re-created my attitude in some pretty profound ways.

Maybe everything we work at has the ability to bring refreshment and re-creation if we have the right perspective and take the time to notice what is happening. The possibility for redemption is all around us.

SPIRITUAL AMNESIA

Thinking back to our predisposition to earn our worth by *doing* — to work hard for status, love, acceptance, and value — I want to remind us that in the beginning of God's story, God created humans in his own image on the sixth day, to *be* like him. The next day — the very first full twenty-four hours of life for Adam and Eve — was a day off. A day of rest.

> By the seventh day God had finished the work he had been doing; so on the seventh day he rested from all his work. Then God blessed the seventh day and made it holy, because on it he rested from all the work of creating that he had done.[1]

In Exodus 20, when God gives the fourth of the Ten Commandments, "Remember the Sabbath day by keeping it holy,"[2] a whole paragraph is provided for this command while the others are just mentioned briefly, such as, "You shall not steal." It seems God knew that we were going to want to work hard at earning and providing for ourselves, and that we would need a rhythm of reminders to help us restore balance and trust in him each week. God created everything, including us, pronounced it good, and then took a break to enjoy it all. That is his desire for us too — to live in a rhythm of resting in his finished work.

So why do we so often treat this command of God's as a suggestion? "Oh, um, yeah ... I really need to do that more. In the New Year, I am going to rest and take some time off. At least I hope to."

We would never say that about any of the other commands: "Next month I am going to cut my stealing and telling lies in half. I really need to." Or "I should definitely stop murdering people. I really gotta cut back."

What?

Why is it that when it comes to the command to rest and then work out of that restored understanding of who we are and who God is, we so easily blow this one off? Maybe we get so busy we forget. We lose track of God's ongoing goodness and provision, and we begin thinking that we are our own source of talent, energy, skills, and — well, everything.

REST AND CREATE

The transformed life offers a perpetual state of sabbath, nonstop resting in Christ's completed work. On the cross, Jesus secured for us what we never could earn for ourselves, the forgiveness of sins and the restoration of our relationship with his Father. We can do nothing to add to this any more than we can cause plants to grow, control the weather, or cause God to love us any more than he already does.

Because of Jesus we can rest. Today. Every day. At a soul level.

Among our church family, we have found it helpful to think of this rhythm as Re-Create: we **Rest** in Jesus' completed work on our behalf, and out of that rest we **Create** value and beauty, and go to work, clean the house, or cook a meal without feeling the need to earn God's (or anyone else's) approval. We already have his approval!

To get into this rhythm, like anything that is important, we simply need to begin.

Rest then work. *Before you leave for work, or as you start your day, spend a little time reminding yourself of what is true of you in Christ — you are dearly loved by the Father.*

Rest while working. *Remember throughout your day that your performance is not what earns God's favor — you already have it because of Jesus!*

Rest from work. *At the end of the day prayerfully thank God for all that happened — leaving everything else in his care.*

Start by setting aside regular times, scheduled if necessary, to rest and refocus on God and his goodness. Put it in your calendar if you must. I do.

NO RESERVATIONS

The temperature was probably around forty-three degrees on the coast. Even though the sun was not shining and the drizzle and wind would not let up, several of my brothers and sisters in the community just *had* to get into the water. "We can't come here and not swim!" they said. So we all ran down to the edge of the water ready to jump into the surf — but the tide was out and the water was a good hundred yards from the edge of the rocky beach where we now stood shivering. Everyone ran through the mucky, slimy beach residue and sort of dove into the surf that was way out there — for about ten seconds. And then everyone ran back as fast as they could. Everyone except me, that is. I was the self-appointed cameraman that day. No polar bear action for me. We went back and jumped into a hot tub set at 104 degrees and slowly warmed up.

We had all come ready to celebrate the past year together in community, a year filled with growth in our relationships and growth in Christ. The next few days in our rented beach home were filled with — well, whatever came up. I love a schedule that has no agenda and no demands, appointments, or reminders needed. We enjoyed one another. We told stories of how we met this person from the group, or the time when God did this or that for one of us. We rehearsed his grace as we prepared meals together with everyone pitching in or offering a favorite recipe. We laughed, drank some wine, prayed together, and discussed what the future held for our missional community.

We all had come straight from a crazy, busy workweek, and we left our weekend together rested and reminded of God's care through this community. We were accepted and loved — even through our differences (and believe me, they exist!). We were re-created, just a little more — again — in the image of a good and glorious God.

I hope everyone will notice. I know I do.

PRESS PAUSE

Sometimes living in this rhythm of Re-Create is caught in snatches. Other times it consists of set-aside, planned times to rest. I think both are needed. I find that the longer, more intentional times I set aside help recalibrate my heart to live in a more constant awareness of God's presence and be able to stay in "rest mode" throughout my normal day.

I find that as long as I am not doing the kind of work that I do throughout most of the week (list stuff), I can find rest and restoration in almost anything. It is important to get out of the office, away from work, chores, parenting duties, or whatever your normal work/performance treadmill may include.

I love working with my hands and getting a little dirty, so physical labor can actually be a very restful thing for me. Working on my Harley, for example, is a total brain-level, heart-level rest for me, and riding the thing with a couple of close friends with no agenda other than to rest, be together, and have fun re-creates me perhaps better than anything else. As I mentioned earlier, sometimes just working in the garden for a while really makes a difference.

For my wife, Tina, making an elaborate breakfast for our kids, friends, and neighbors re-creates her soul. There are no picture-perfect presentations or expensive menu items, just lots of pancakes, salami eggs (the best thing ever!), a few mimosas, and no set schedule. She reconnects to God and his generosity as she shares it with others.

Many of my friends in the community have worked to create small pockets of time to re-create in their normal days. Josh gets up thirty minutes before he needs to get ready for work to get his heart ready for the day by a simple time of reading his Bible, some inspirational thoughts to remind him of God and his greatness, or a few minutes in prayer talking to his "Daddy" in heaven. Doing this aligns his heart with God's before heading off into the fray. He'll also try to find another thirty-minute chunk during the day before pressing into the afternoon or evening.

Heather grabs moments to re-create herself as her children nap or play throughout the day. "I watch my children as they create things," she says. "It just comes natural for them to take a random group of objects and make them into something amazing to them. When I stop to notice, it helps me to do the same thing — see the activities in my day all coming together as a part of God's larger plan for things and people around me."

RE-CREATE

I am superthankful for the times I have had to spend long, unin-
terrupted times alone, hanging out with God and just listening.
Even now, as I am writing this chapter, I am alone, sitting on a boat
owned by my friends Mark and Roseanne. It is a real blessing: a
three-bedroom cabin cruiser big enough to sleep eight and go
anywhere in the world. I just like to sit and watch the seagulls or
stand on the deck and look at the other boats come and go. After
a few hours of quieting my heart, listening without speaking, finding solitude for my ears and my mind, I notice something. I relax.
Really relax. A different posture seems to come over me — a grand
aaahhh releases from deep within — and a refreshed, "slower-
paced Caesar" begins to climb up out of the pile of meetings, travel,
and deadlines.

How do *you* re-create?

BUT SOMETIMES IT'S HARD …

Okay, I am going to just come right out and admit it — I *suck* at this
rhythm! It is hard to live in a moment-by-moment reality of sabbath rest, and it is hard to set aside a regular time each week to be
restored and refocused on Christ.

The Israelites thought that the Sabbath was purely about *not* working — but they missed the whole point of it. The reason God wanted
people to stop *doing* stuff for a day, in rhythm, was so that they
would be renewed and transformed by focusing on his work and
creativity and power. His intent was not just that we would take a
short break, or even a day off of work, but ultimately that our hearts
would be refocused on the gospel reality of who God is and what
has been accomplished in Christ. So don't let resting or re-creating
become a new law to be observed. *I have to work harder at resting!*
That doesn't really make sense, does it? Ask God to cultivate the
desire for re-creation in your heart, by his Spirit. You can't muster
it up on your own, but God can *create* it within you. That's his job.

The point of this rhythm is not immobility or mindless amusement and entertainment. It is to intentionally spend time regularly realigning our hearts with God's heart.

Twentieth-century American pastor and preacher A. W. Tozer once said, "I can tell how much God you have by how much entertainment you need." The word *amuse* is made up of two parts: the prefix *a* meaning "no, without, absence of," and the word *muse*, a noun referring to the source of one's inspiration, which as a verb means "to be absorbed in thought or focus." A-musement, then, is to stop thinking or focusing on anything as a source of inspiration. Amusement is the exact opposite of what we are talking about. Living in this rhythm of re-creation is choosing to live focused on God's great provision so that we can truly rest and find a peace that far exceeds mindless televised entertainment or games.

GIVE ME A BREAK!

Self-focus as a major character quality or lifestyle is one thing; an obedient response to live in a rhythm of allowing ourselves to be re-created by God is another. If we are not rested — physically, emotionally, and spiritually — then we won't do a very good job of serving others. Our motivation will be off. We'll have every excuse in the book why we either can't serve others or why we can't stop and rest — or both. God understood this. If we *never* focus on ourselves, our care, our re-creation, then our focus ends up on ourselves *a lot* of the time.

I am so tired. I am so busy. I am so me . . . me . . . my world . . . me . . . *Whoa!*

Stop already. Rest.

Wouldn't it be great if every encounter we had with another person served as a reminder to them that God is big enough. That he is enough for their job, family, relational or health challenges — whatever they are facing. How can we tell our neighbors, or anyone who does not know Jesus, that we have an amazing Father and that Jesus has provided for us in astounding ways, yet live fast-paced, freaked-out, frenetic lives? No one will believe us. But if we live in a rhythm of resting in God's all-encompassing provision and then creating good and value and beauty, others will be influenced by our lives and drawn to us. They will want to know why we can live in the middle of the same apparent storms they live in and have such peace.

PRESS PLAY

This idea of Re-Create carries with it a sense of playfulness too. Do we take time to play? My buddy Jeff told me once that he could tell if his heart was truly at rest when he could slow down enough to play with his kids. (By the way, he told me that he hates Chutes and Ladders because the only way to win is by luck of the draw. What does that say about his heart?) Anyway, he has realized that God will continue to run the world without him for a while as he spends time just *being* with his kids and having fun.

What would it look like if God came and ran your life for a day? Everything — your thoughts, words, actions, choices, every conversation, every hope or plan made. Do you think it would go better than if you were running things? I bet it would.

God: "I can handle all of this just fine on my own, thank you."

Us: "No, thank you, Dad!"

As we live out our identity as missionaries, we can rest and play with those whom God has brought into our lives. Playing in the way the culture plays can be both a time of rest and an opportunity to grow closer to others. Often it can provide ways to serve or bless someone else as well, while we find those times amazingly refreshing and restorative too.

After trying to explain this to my brother-in-law Dave, all of a sudden the lightbulb went on for him, and his eyes went very wide. "So I can go out golfing or riding with my buddy on Sunday morning," he said, "relaxing and spending time with him as an act of obedience and worship?"

Yes, Dave. You get to.

BIG E ON THE EYE CHART

In some ways, re-creation is the most important of all the rhythms to cultivate. If our hearts are not centered on God and his provision, then they are centered on us and our own abilities, strength, and resources. Jesus said, "If you remain in me and I in you, you will bear much fruit; apart from me you can do nothing."[3]

We need new hearts, new rhythms that both remind us and demonstrate to others that our God is worthy to be trusted. It is the cultivation of this rhythm that can move our hearts to live like this as a way of life. Continuously.

Just as we will in heaven for eternity.

THINGS TO THINK ABOUT

How conditioned are you to believe the do = be lie? Do you feel like you are on a treadmill at times?

Do you find it hard to rest — truly let down and *be*? Why?

What are the most restful and restorative activities in your life? Could they become a rhythm or pattern?

In what ways are these restorative things a picture of the way God originally created the world and people to be?

ALMOST THERE

I hope you are beginning to get a picture of how our new, transformed lives are meant to be lived. Our gospel identity can be expressed a million different yet natural ways in the normal rhythms of everyday life — a single life, not a divided one, living out what is now true of us.

Now let's look at a family in my community that shows the natural flow of our transformed identity worked out through the rhythms, and how this natural flow can lead to growth and new life for others. I'll tell you their story and give you a better idea of how all of these rhythms fit together for them as they make disciples in their own neighborhood.

Chapter 13

ONE LIFE TO LIVE

*Living our transformed identity in
the rhythms of everyday life.*

EACH OF US has the same twenty-four hours each day, seven days each week. It's just enough time to jam all of life into and then start again next week. I have learned that it is not life lived as God's family of missionary servants, empowered by the Holy Spirit for his mission, that burns people out or causes them to want to throw in the towel of faith. It is when we believe the lie that says we can continue building our own version of the American Dream life (or European Dream life or wherever), pursuing a bigger house, nicer cars, better vacations, the best of everything — *and* try and fit in a little "church" or "ministry" that life gets out of whack.

We have been given just one life to live. We cannot live two different existences. In fact, any life we try and build around *me* at the center is no life at all. That is why Jesus said, "If you try to keep your life for yourself, you will lose it. But if you give up your life for me, you will find true life."[1] Living our lives as the family of God on his mission is the life we were created to live. That is *truly* life.

IF I'VE HEARD IT ONCE …

I had just returned home to Tacoma after speaking at a conference in Colorado. Other than the low-grade headache I felt from being a mile higher in altitude than I am used to, I had a great time being with saints who were beginning to believe a better story, one in which they have been given a new identity. We talked about many of the same things you've read so far, and I told a lot of the stories I have shared here. What is interesting to me is that wherever I go in America or overseas and talk about this lifestyle, the following comments and questions always come up:

> "This all sounds amazing to me, and I really do believe this is true of us if we're Christians, but how in the world do I fit all of this 'missionary stuff' into my life? I already feel so busy and, frankly, a little overwhelmed!"
> "I thought that only people who worked full-time for a church did these kinds of things and lived this way — and probably only in other countries, right?"
> "We're just an average family living a normal life, so how would we even start to find others who want to live as a family of missionary servants?"

I know many people with similar questions. Seth and Stacy McBee, friends of mine who live near Seattle, were asking the same things a few years ago. Their story shows the natural flow and integration of all of the four aspects of our transformed identity — family, missionaries, servants, disciples — worked out through the six rhythms — story-formed, listening, eating, blessing, celebrating, and re-creating. It will help put all the pieces of the puzzle together for us.

Seth grew up a third-or-fourth-generation Christian. His father was a pastor, his grandparents were missionaries out of the country, and everyone in his life went to church on Sundays. Stacy was raised in a family that did not believe in God and rarely went to church except for weddings and funerals. Occasionally a

Christmas Eve or Easter service was thrown in as "fire insurance." She came to faith just out of high school, and the two met and got married a few years later. Shortly after having their first child, a son, they built the perfect little house on the perfect little suburban cul-de-sac and got to work finding a perfect little church to attend.

They landed in a congregation that was more than happy to have two new busy beavers who were anxious to serve. Within six months of them being there, the elders asked Seth if he would be the youth pastor. He wasn't specially trained for this, and the role came with no pay or benefits, but he gladly accepted the opportunity. He liked the work and the prestige that came along with being on the *inside* track with the rest of the leadership team at the church. He figured he could fit the responsibilities of the position in around his responsibilities at home and at his business, which he needed to run in order to make a living and feed his family.

THESE FOUR WALLS

It wasn't very long before Seth and Stacy were spending ginormous amounts of time at the church building. The senior pastor's wife and the other women in the church made it clear that Stacy was to be there with her husband, showing support and helping out with the ministry a lot. She was now pregnant with their second child and dragging two-year-old Cole around to everything they did.

It seemed that Seth and Stacy were always doing something church related. On Thursdays they would spend the entire day and evening at the building, involved in MOPS, AWANA, and the evening program with the youth group. Sunday was filled with services and other leadership activities. There were Bible studies to lead, volunteers to organize, special holiday outreach activities to plan and execute. At one point, Seth added it up and realized there had been only four days that month when he had not been at the church building doing something.

So much for seeking and saving the lost in their neighborhood — there was no time!

Seth and Stacy began to feel that running programs was taking precedent over growth in the good news of the gospel and being with not-yet believers. The demands of their growing family and business were mounting, and the pull to *do church* seemed endless. Legalism grew in Seth's heart as he focused more and more on sinning less and working harder — and he wanted everyone around him, including Stacy and the kids, to do the same. Something had to change. *Is this the life that Jesus died on a cross to give us?* they wondered.

The final straw for Stacy came one day when she showed up at the Sunday service with a throbbing migraine headache and two very young kids in strollers. She was just happy to have made it there and for them all to be wearing clothes! Never mind that her hair looked like something had caught fire earlier that morning. (Is that a little piece of toast in there?) One of the other pastors' wives came up and said to her, "You look a little frazzled today, Stacy." She explained that she had had a pretty rough morning. Seth had come in hours earlier to lead Sunday school, and she had to get the kids ready for church by herself while fighting nausea. This woman then looked knowingly, fearfully, and yet somewhat judgmentally at Stacy and said, "Well, just make sure you keep it together while you're here at church this morning."

That was it for Stacy. She was done pretending everything was okay. She was done raising her kids inside the four walls of that building, and she was ready to be done with "church" forever. She loved Jesus and wanted to love people more, but this was definitely not working.

NOW WHAT?

Around that same time, Seth began to grow in his awareness of what grace looked like. He saw how Jesus' life, death, and resurrection had earned God's perfect acceptance for him, Stacy, and *everyone* who believed. He began to back off of the legalism, and his teaching and preaching began to shift toward good news versus trying harder. He challenged the other pastors and leaders to get rid of some of the programs and endless classes they held weekly at the church and instead intentionally lead people to love their neighbors, living out their faith. His challenge was met with great and unfortunate resistance. "We are not changing a thing here; this is the way we have done things for years. Our people want and need these things."

Their hearts were broken. Should they just suck it up and keep quiet? They felt they just had to pursue a more authentic Christian life — or die trying. Eventually they found their way into a new group of believers who were part of an emerging Soma church in their area. I remember meeting Seth not long after they started hanging around. He was confused and excited at the same time. Hearing everyone talk about life in community and how the teaching emphasized God's grace made the two of them realize that they were not completely crazy after all. "We found our tribe," they said, "our people!"

DRAW ON THE MAP AS YOU GO

Seth knew they had to start living as missionaries in their own neighborhood. But there was one problem. Not long after he had moved into his new home, Seth had gone around knocking on doors "evangelizing" everyone. He would ask them a series of questions he had learned from a book and sort of trick people into admitting they had lied at some point in their lives and probably stolen at least something small — maybe something like a pen or paper clip from work. He then quoted a few verses from the Bible, declaring that if they didn't believe in Jesus, they were going to go straight to hell. After all, they were confessing liars and thieves.

Pretty rough.

Now while there is some degree of truth in this — we will in fact have to answer for the sins we have committed in our lives — this was not a well-received way of helping folks come to know the loving pursuit of God and his Son, Jesus. Most people gave Seth the ol' "thanks but no thanks" and slammed the door in his face.

Seth came to me and asked what he should do to get started on a better foot. I told him I had no idea and suggested he start by praying with Stacy and asking the Holy Spirit, "What next?" He told me my answer was a little underwhelming. But I was thankful that I had not given this reforming legalist a missional "to-do" list. He would have gone hard after it but never stopped to ask God about any of it. Later he told me that the Holy Spirit had always felt sort of like the weird uncle of the Trinity to him, not really a part of his thinking about God, Jesus, or his faith. But they decided to try it, offering up a halfhearted prayer: "Okay, Spirit, um, can you tell us what's next with our neighbors? We really do want to figure out how to love them and show them who you truly are. If you can just give us that first step, we'll try not to bother you too much."

Amazingly, within a day or two, independently of each other, both Seth and Stacy felt like the Spirit was telling them to do something kind of strange. They heard that still, small voice inside saying they were to move their barbecue grill from around back in their fenced yard and start grilling on Friday evenings out front on the driveway. "Okay, God, it sounds crazy, but here we go." And guess what? That first Friday, as the smells of grilled burgers, brats, and veggies made their way into the neighborhood, people started stopping by to talk and see what was going on. (Why should this seem surprising?) Seth invited everyone who stopped to grab some food and join them — right there on the driveway in front of the garage. He started conversations with an apology for not having been a very good neighbor.

"We have lived here for four or five years now," he said, "and I don't even know your names. I'm really sorry." Everyone was very gracious and confessed they had not done any better at the "good neighbor thing." They also said that they *loved* getting to know others and hoped that Seth would do this again soon.

Something quite spiritual, maybe even supernatural, took place that day in suburbia. Seth and Stacy came to believe that God actually spoke to them, and the people around them began to see a picture of God's kingdom breaking into their mundane routine. Jesus taught us that his kingdom is like a great feast where everyone gets invited to participate. This was, for many, their first invitation to the Party!

Seth and Stacy started having these out-in-the-driveway cookouts every other week after that. Seth set up a Facebook page for all the neighbors to stay in touch. They used this to post needs that came up, invite each other to parties that were spontaneously erupting, and generally have fun together.

HUNGRY FOR MORE

Around this same time, Seth had invited a few other couples from Soma to join him on mission to make disciples in his neighborhood. They brainstormed and prayed about what they should do next to engage more deeply in relationships. It was decided that in a few weeks, on the Fourth of July, they would throw the 1st Annual Wiffle Ball Tournament and Chili Cook-Off. They made simple flyers and handed them out door-to-door to all 153 homes in their subdivision. They had a lot of fun that day. Everyone was surprised at how many people came out to take a swat at that little plastic ball — ten teams and over 250 people hanging out together! (Maybe it was because of the trophies they handed out at the end for the winning teams.)

After that day, a lot more people started showing up for the Friday night barbecues. Seth, Stacy, and the others from their missional community started very intentionally spending more and more of their time having different families over for dinner and going out on date nights together. Clearly several couples were beginning to really lean in to relationship with them and were even open to having spiritual discussions in light of what they saw and experienced with the people in this unique "family."

As the season turned to fall then winter, Seth and Stacy knew that their outside grilling was soon going to come to an end.

Aah, but they had heard about others doing breakfast clubs, and decided to give that a try — but with their own twist. Instead of serving standard breakfast fare (eggs, bacon, pancakes, etc.), they offered a unique Danish breakfast pastry called *aebleskivers*, which are made fresh in a special cast-iron pan. These amazing balls of flaky goodness were filled each week with a different fruit, cheese, or whatever they dreamed up. The kids loved them. The parents loved them. What's not to love about an aebleskiver?

HEY, GOD … IT'S US AGAIN

Seth and Stacy began to pray and ask God to guide them to have the right conversations leading up to inviting some of these friends and neighbors to join them in going through the Story of God together. Incredibly — and everyone in their group experienced this — all sorts of spiritual conversations started popping up. People began asking them questions:

"You used to be a pastor or something, right? Tell me about that and why you no longer do that."

"Your marriage looks different than ours or my parents' did growing up. Is this due to your faith?"

God was answering their simple prayers as his Spirit guided things along. He was perfectly guiding these questions, conversations, and relationships toward his story.

Stacy told me that at this point her heart was challenged a little.
Okay, a lot. Up until now, they had been hanging out and building
relationships with everyone outside in the front yard or at the park.
Outside. Outside of *her home*. Now they were coming *inside* her
little sanctuary! Someone in the community reminded her that we
are to find our ultimate refuge and rest in Christ, not in the things
he gives us to enjoy. Yep, they were right; she believed that with
her head and asked God to make that real in her heart as well.

He did, and over the next several weeks — graciously, naturally, as
trust was built — five families and their children from the neighborhood decided they wanted to go through the Story together with
Seth and the others to get their questions answered. And they met
inside Stacy's home to do it.

Nerd alert: Seth and the others never used the term "missional
community" when talking with their neighbors. That is how they
view themselves in light of their true identity, but they would not
say things to their new friends like, "Hey, do you want to come
over and eat with my missional community?" Or "Do you want to
do this Bible study thing with my missional community?" They just
built normal friendships with people as they served, loved, and
cared for them, and then they naturally invited them to participate
in this fun activity or this meaningful story experience together.
They did not make any one activity or event the be-all and end-all
for everybody.

The weeks flew by as they listened to and talked through God's
story together, sharing their own stories along the way. It was
remarkable how they came to really love one another, growing in
their patience and care as they learned everyone's background
and life experiences. This group of friends was becoming a close
family. They started serving the needs of anyone as they came
up — and not just theirs, but those of anyone in the neighborhood.

When Marin, who lives around their corner, was sick and unable
to drive for months, Stacy would call her up to see how she could

help. "I'm over here at the grocery store; do you need anything while I'm here?" Little things done in rhythm over time can make a big impact. Marin was a Wiccan who followed modern pagan practices in several areas of her life. But she was so overwhelmed by the love that Stacy and the others from her missional community showed her, that when a close friend of hers was in need, she called to see if they could help her too.

"A friend of mine called, and her husband just left her permanently. She has no way to buy Christmas presents for their children. Do you think you guys could help me help her?" The community all jumped in, no strings attached, and took care of it.

Seth told me, "Actually, when you are thinking and living like a family of missionary servants, things like this are prime opportunities served up on a platter by God. We just helped her to be a blessing to someone she cares about. Now she's starting to understand what we mean by 'blessed to be a blessing.' I'm glad we didn't miss that one!"

YES, WE GET TO

It didn't happen overnight, but it hadn't been that long either, when three people from Seth and Stacy's missional community decided they wanted to follow Jesus. After spending time going through the Story of God and living with Seth's "family" for several months, they wanted to continue to walk in his ways and be baptized.

[*Record scratch noise here*]

Wait a second. Stop the music. Could it really be that this couple, who used to spend half of their waking hours inside the walls of a church building "doing ministry stuff" and never making a single disciple, had now partnered with God to host barbecues, throw parties, and tell stories — and *now* they were going to be baptizing new believers? Were they actually making disciples, right here, in their everyday life?

Yes.

How did they *possibly* fit all of this into their already busy lives? Seth still had a business to run. Stacy was now at home with two young kids and another on the way. The others in their missional community were also busy suburban professionals with kids and families and hobbies. How could this be?

ONE LIFE TO LIVE. REALLY.

Here are some of the things that filled a normal, average week of Seth and Stacy's lives as this family on mission all got rolling: Everyone in their group made a list of different friends they were praying for and believed God wanted them to pursue in relationship for his glory and their discipleship. They looked for opportunities to have someone or a couple over for dinner once or twice each week. Stacy hates to cook, so she didn't do anything fancy or elaborate. In fact, they purposely wanted to avoid making these meals feel like a big production and something that others felt obligated to reciprocate. They just wanted regular family dinner nights with a couple of friends added into the rhythm of normal life. "Hey, we were thinking of ordering a few pizzas and throwing a movie in for the kids. Do you guys want to come over and join us?" Instead of freaking out and trying to be the perfect cook or homemaker, Stacy was learning to relax, have fun, and make others the focus of her intention, not the dust bunnies that were scurrying around the dining room.

Since Seth and Stacy had adopted the habit of grilling their dinners out in front of the house, a fair number of impromptu parties happened, with friends just stopping by for dinner. "Hey, are you guys gonna be barbecuing tonight? Cool. We'll go grab some burgers and be right back."

Stacy found that almost any day of the week she could call or text a few of the other stay-at-home moms in the area and invite them out for a quick coffee. "Hey, I was thinking of taking the baby for a walk in the stroller up to the café. I'm leaving in thirty minutes — you want to go with us?" Instead of staying home every day in her comfy sweatpants, she intentionally spends time out with others as time allows. (Okay, sometimes she's out there in those same sweats!)

Instead of packing their kids in the car on weekends and holidays, heading off to go do whatever they felt like doing, they began spending more of their time in the neighborhood where others hung out and played. There was always someone out fixing something in the yard or a soccer game to go and cheer on. Unplanned opportunities to be together always came up.

Their kids played sports with other children in the neighborhood, so this became another easy rhythm to get into. Seth posted on Facebook that he was going to start coaching the five- and six-year-olds' soccer team at the park. Others from his missional community who had kids the same age purposely placed their kids on his team so that they easily had at least two more times each week to hang out with their neighbors. That also made it simple for follow-up victory trips to the ice cream parlor or pizza place. Seth did the same thing during basketball season. He and Stacy figured, *Our kids are in these sports anyway — we want to support them in it — why not just make it all a part of our missional rhythm?*

When another mom who lived around the corner had surgery and was put on complete bed rest for several weeks, Stacy would go and pick up her laundry, bring it home, wash, dry, and fold it for her, and then return it. During the times spent picking it up and dropping it off, they had great conversations together. Stacy did most of this laundry at times when her little ones were napping and she needed to be at home, a nice little bit of redeemed time for mission. "All we really do is treat people like they are our family," Stacy told me, "looking out for each other, noticing needs, taking the time to care."

A favorite rhythm for Seth, one he borrowed from our friend Todd and that I mentioned earlier, is when he and a few of the guys in his missional community sit on the porch and smoke their pipes. Other men from the neighborhood, smelling the smoke wafting through their yards, find them and join in. At times they will have up to ten guys all sitting together on the porch, packing their pipes and talking about every imaginable topic. It is during these impromptu activities that friendships are built. Questions come up that demand a gospel explanation. This is what life together in community looks like.

Seth and Stacy have begun to lead others to walk in the ways of Jesus in their own context, in very ordinary ways. A common week may include a couple of meals with friends, maybe a pipe night, a few errands done together, and a group service project on the weekend. Watching movies, taking the kids to the park or a museum, and making phone calls to check in on people are all common. They'll get to the gym three times a week with other guys and gals, both believers and not-yet believers who are being discipled. Catch the rhythm?

Right now, I'll bet some of you are thinking, *Hey, all of this is just normal stuff!*

That's the point: normal but intentional.

At first, Seth and Stacy initiated most of these gatherings and happenings with others. They hosted the majority of the cookouts and various activities, but over time others picked up on acting as hosts, and today people are hanging out all around the neighborhood. The kingdom of God was breaking into their lives. Trust was replacing fear; self-interest was being exchanged for generosity. A light began to shine that was unavoidable and completely attractive to everyone.

"We have the best neighborhood in the world!" people began to say. They claimed that Seth and Stacy were the reason why this was all happening, but the two were quick to tell them that Jesus was doing all this, that he loves them, that he loves their neighborhood, and that he wants them to know what it looks like to follow him instead of empty religion.

In Seth's own words, "Our lives have little by little become intertwined with the folks in our missional community and those Jesus has given us to love and disciple to faith in him. This is not something that we 'add on' to our days; it is who we are and how we live. We can't imagine ever *not* living like this anymore. It is part of our identity. We could never go back to just merely attending a church service for an hour or two on Sunday morning and then living for ourselves throughout the week. That's not what it means to be a Christian. We're disciples! We want to live more and more like Jesus. Right here. In fact, I can't believe we *get to* live this way!"

BUT SOMETIMES IT'S HARD …

You need to know that we have a powerful enemy who does not want us to live a missional lifestyle. Satan will attack our health, marriages, children, confidence, and faith to get us to go back to living life primarily focused on self. This was the case for Seth and Stacy, and one of these attacks came as a knock on the door. A neighbor who lives literally ten feet away next door, someone they had been tirelessly reaching out to, trying to show Jesus to his whole family, came over on a Friday when he knew Seth would be at work.

For twenty minutes, he cussed at Stacy, saying he had put up with her for eight years but in reality had hated her the entire time. He then listed off ways in which he found her to be disgusting.

Stacy called Seth in tears to let him know what happened. As her husband, Seth was furious. Would he blow up at the guy? Should he punch his lights out? He called the man, and as they spoke, Seth called out his lies where they needed to be called out. In the end, he told him that they would respect his wishes for their families not to interact further, but it was not what he and Stacy wanted. They loved this man and his family. So sad.

When this happened, Seth and Stacy's first thought was, *Why?* If they listed off all the ways they had loved this family over the years, you'd think they were making it up. It was a reminder that we should never be loving others for what we'll get from them or how they will ultimately respond, but only because of how much our Father has loved us. Now they have to pray about new ways to express love to this neighbor — but it is hard. They have to remind themselves that this man is not their enemy. We can often treat the very people God has called us to serve and love as an adversary because they disagree with or reject us. When this happens, we need to be reminded of the truth.

> Our struggle is not against flesh and blood *(people)*, but against the rulers, against the authorities, against the powers of this dark world and against the spiritual forces of evil in the heavenly realms *(Satan and his demons)*."[2]

Love your neighbor. Hate the Enemy.

As you begin to live your life on mission, showing others what God is like, be ready. Satan is prowling around like a roaring lion, looking for someone to devour.[3] And when you're breaking into the world around you with the beauty of God's kingdom, that someone is you.

A GLORIOUS MESS

I hope Seth and Stacy's story excites you and has helped show the typical rhythms of some regular people who are living out their new identity in Christ. This lifestyle is not perfect; in fact, it's supermessy! But messed-up people make good soil for the seed of the gospel to grow in because there is a lot of fertilizer in their lives.[4] All of us have things that God is working out, and he seems to fill our lives with people who have needs just like us.

This life together is not turned on like a light switch. A life that is full of people and mission doesn't happen instantly. It takes time and patience, beginning by being patient with yourself! And where you are on this journey is exactly where you're supposed to be.

Most of us were not raised in a missional lifestyle, even if we grew up in Christian homes. No one ever told us that we could live like missionaries right where we are. It takes time to grow into this way of life, to come to a fuller belief of who God has made us to be, allowing his transformation to creep into all the folds of our hearts and lives.

One part of our lives after the next will be turned over to the truth — new identity, new rhythms, empowered and led by the Spirit.

THINGS TO THINK ABOUT

What are you feeling after reading about living life as a family of missionary servants?

What is shifting in your heart and mind concerning who you are and how you *get* to live?

What parts of Seth and Stacy's story are most attractive to you? Which are scariest?

What do you still wonder about after reading this book?

Others may be asking the same questions — or have a few answers for you from their experiences. Go to www.gcmcollective.org to find thousands of people who are on this same journey.

EPILOGUE

Beginning to believe . . .

WE HAVE BEEN GIVEN this crazy life to live in all the glory and adventure that only a good God like ours could dream up. Will you believe that what I have said and what the Bible teaches about this transformed life is true?

I hope you will. Because a life like this starts by believing the truth.

It may feel at times like this has not happened for you or that you're moving backward in some area of your life. Even after reading all of this and hearing these stories, you may be suffering from a case of the *yabotts* (pronounced "yeah, but . . .").

"Do you believe that you are part of God's family and he loves you regardless of any of your past?"

"Yeah, but I'm still a mess. . . ."

"Do you believe that Jesus has sent you, indwelt by his own Spirit, to bring others into this family?"

"Yeah, but I don't know where to start. . . ."

Or perhaps the habits of sin and self-focused patterns, many of which are completely supported by our culture — and sometimes even by our churches — may be pulling you back to live for your own glory, ease, and comfort.

Let me remind you, if you have put your faith and life in the hands of Jesus and begun to walk with him, you *have* been transformed. Fling yourself into this truth. Jesus is bringing about your maturity, and it is his work to bring you fully into his likeness. He'll grab ahold of the weakest parts of your life, the most fragile aspects of your faith, making them the strongest. He is also using the worst parts of your life as opportunities for his grace to shine and show others this beautiful transformation.

Your life is part of a much bigger plan. So many others whom you love, whom God has brought into your life, desperately need this transformation too. Tell them about your new identity and how you are learning to live in light of the truth. Tell them about Jesus and who they are meant to be. They need him, and he is worthy of their worship. Jesus gave everything that they might have life and have it to the fullest, that they might be transformed into his likeness and walk with him and his Father in a life that is complete and everlasting.

You are a part of that journey. Go after it. This is the beginning of something big!

I hope to run into you someday, doing all the normal stuff of life, with a bunch of disciples in tow and the Good News just dripping out of your mouth and being proclaimed in every step, bite of food, and breath you take.

And maybe I'll hear you ask the question, "So ... who are *you*?"

THE STORY OF GOD

THIS IS A STORY found in the Bible, about God, a being who has always existed and is the creator of everything. God is the only one in this story who always does what is good, right, and perfect — the Bible calls him holy. While God created the foundations of the earth, angels (his first creation) were there watching. They sang together and worshiped God — but some of these angels rebelled against God and his ways. The Bible teaches that all rebellion against God is called sin. And because of God's holiness, his perfect justice will not allow sin to remain in his presence, so he sent the rebellious angels, now known as demons, down into darkness on the earth.

Then God decided to create another being, called humans, in his own image. God said, "Let us make man in our image to be like us." He then prepared the earth as a place for the humans to live — filling the earth with plants, birds, fish, and animals of all kinds. God created the first humans, Adam and Eve, and placed them in a beautiful garden and trusted them to care for and rule over all of his creation on earth. He told them, "Be fruitful and multiply."

Every day, God would spend time with the humans, walking with them in the cool of the day. He showed them how to live in the best possible way — a life lived close to God and under his protection — a life that is full and complete and eternal. God looked at all that he had created and saw that it was *very good*!

Unfortunately, Adam and Eve eventually chose to rebel against God and his authority, choosing to live in their own ways instead of his. Since God will not allow evil and rebellion to remain in his presence, Adam and Eve were sent out of the garden, away from God. Separated from God and no longer following his ways, they became subject to sickness, pain, and death. God told them, "The way you have chosen to live will bring you great struggles and pain, and then you will return to the ground from which you came." Not only were these humans now separated from God because of their sin, but they would also suffer death as they were separated from the Giver of Life.

After leaving the garden, the number of humans on earth grew rapidly. Sin spread from Adam and Eve to their sons, and it continued to spread from generation to generation. Even though humans were created in God's image, everyone chose to disobey God. They all constantly acted out in violence against one another. This went on for thousands of years.

Then God established a special relationship and a covenant promise — representing the deepest of all agreements — with a man named Abraham. God told Abraham, "I'll make you the father of a great nation and famous throughout history. I will bless those who bless you and curse those who curse you. The entire earth will be blessed through your descendants. I will always be your God and you will always be my people."

Abraham's family, called the Israelites, were to be a new kind of people who would show the world what it means to once again live in God's ways. God gave them a vast amount of land where they enjoyed his blessings as they grew into a large nation.

But as time went by, the Israelites began doing what was right in their own eyes and rebelled against God and his laws. They stopped trusting in God and worshiped idols — people, things, wealth, and power — over God. In their rebellion, the Israelites faced great struggles and ended up a defeated nation of slaves. But God continued to love his people and promised that one day one of their descendants would come to rescue and restore humanity, and all of creation, back to the way God originally created it.

Then there were four hundred years of silence between God and his people.

The Israelites, called Jews, had been under the control of other nations for hundreds of years, and they were now ruled by Rome, the most powerful empire the world had ever known.

Finally, God sent an angel to a young woman named Mary in the town of Nazareth. The angel appeared to her and said, "You will become pregnant and have a son and you are to name him Jesus. He will become a king whose kingdom will never end! This will happen supernaturally by God's Spirit, so this baby will be called God's Son."

God revealed to Mary and her soon-to-be-husband, Joseph, that this boy was the long awaited Messiah King, the one whom God promised he'd send to rescue his people! Sure enough, the next year Mary gave birth to a son whom she named Jesus, which means "the God who saves." Jesus grew up in both height and wisdom, and was loved by God and everyone who knew him. He lived a remarkable life, always choosing to live in God's ways and do what was good, right, and perfect.

As a man, Jesus called people to follow him, inviting them to be a part of what he called the kingdom of God, calling people to once again live under God's rule and reign. He said, "God blesses those who realize their need for him; the humble and poor, the gentle and merciful — the kingdom of God belongs to them. God blesses the pure in heart and those who hunger and thirst to be with him."

He taught people that the kingdom of God is within us, in our heart and minds.

He said, "God showed his great love for people by sending me — his only Son — to this world. Anyone who believes in me and lives in my ways will find life that is complete and eternal! He sent me here to save people — not to judge them. Those who want to live in sin and darkness will reject me and bring God's judgment on themselves. But those who want to live in God's ways will trust me and live forever!"

As God had promised, he sent Jesus to rescue humanity from sin and the penalty of death. God accepted Jesus' perfect life in place of our own. Jesus was brutally beaten and died painfully on a wooden cross, taking the punishment that all of rebellious humanity deserved! Three days later, Jesus conquered death when God raised him back to life, and he was seen by over five hundred eyewitnesses.

Soon afterward, Jesus went to be with his Father in heaven, rising up into the clouds right before his followers' eyes! He promised that he would send his own Holy Spirit to come and dwell within them. The Spirit would remind them of all Jesus taught, transform their hearts to be like Jesus, and give them power to walk in the ways of God like Jesus did. Jesus also sent his followers to go out and tell others about him — his life and his sacrifice for their sins — and lead them to trust him and walk in his ways.

This was the beginning of what the Bible calls the church, a community of people all over the world who, because of Jesus, once again enjoy a life that is full and complete — living in the ways of God.

We can join this amazing story, for the story continues with us!

The Bible also tells us the end of this story, that Jesus promised to come back one day to destroy all evil, sin, and rebellion. Then there will be no more sickness, pain, or death. God's kingdom will come in fullness, and everyone and everything will live under his rule and be restored back to the way God created them to be.

Until then, we get to live in God's ways, giving people a foretaste of what life is like in the kingdom.

IDENTITY AND RHYTHMS DIAGNOSTIC

HERE ARE A FEW SIMPLE QUESTIONS and ideas you can use for getting started to help tune up your beliefs about your new, transformed identity lived out in everyday rhythms.

Remember, all of this starts in your head, moves to your heart, and then gets lived out through your hands.

WHO WE ARE

FAMILY

Do you know you are a forgiven and dearly loved child who has God as your Father?

> *See what great love the Father has lavished on us, that we should be called children of God! And that is what we are!*
> (1 John 3:1)

Do you understand what you have inherited as a part of this family? *Everything!*

Now if we are children, then we are heirs — heirs of God and co-heirs with Christ. (Romans 8:17)

Are you spending time with others like a healthy family would?

All the believers were together and had everything in common. . . . Every day they continued to meet together in the temple courts. They broke bread in their homes and ate together with glad and sincere hearts. (Acts 2:44,46)

MISSIONARY

Do you know that Jesus has personally sent *you* on his mission?

Jesus said, "Peace be with you! As the Father has sent me, I am sending you." (John 20:21)

Do you believe that Jesus is on this mission with you?

"Surely I am with you always, to the very end of the age." (Matthew 28:20)

Are you increasingly reorienting your life, time, and priorities around the mission?

"If you cling to your life, you will lose it; but if you give up your life for me, you will find it."(Matthew 10:39 *NLT*)

SERVANT

Do you know that Jesus has served *you*, giving everything he had?

God demonstrates his own love for us in this: While we were still sinners, Christ died for us. (Romans 5:8)

Do you believe that Jesus' life, given to us and for us, is enough?

Therefore, since we have been made right in God's sight by faith, we have peace with God because of what Jesus Christ our Lord has done for us. (Romans 5:1 NLT)

In light of the grace we have been shown, are you increasingly laying your preferences and priorities down for the sake of others?

"Greater love has no one than this: to lay down one's life for one's friends." (John 15:13)

DISCIPLE

Do you know that Jesus has called you to follow him and become like him?

Then Jesus said to his disciples, "Whoever wants to be my disciple must deny themselves and take up their cross and follow me." (Matthew 16:24)

Do you believe that Jesus' life has now become your life?

For you died, and your life is now hidden with Christ in God. (Colossians 3:3)

Are you increasingly reorienting the rhythms of your life to make disciples of Jesus by the power of his Spirit?

Be wise in the way you act toward outsiders; make the most of every opportunity. (Colossians 4:5)

HOW WE LIVE

STORY-FORMED

Are you growing in your knowledge of the Bible as one big story?

What is changing for you in light of seeing the big picture of Scripture more clearly?

Who could you begin to go through the Story-Formed Way with in community?

LISTEN

Are you regularly "listening backward" to God through spending time in his Word? Begin with a small, achievable rhythm and grow from there.

When you read from the Bible, ask yourself these three questions:

> What is God saying to me?
> What am I going to do about it?
> Who else in my life would benefit from hearing this too? Go tell them.

Are you beginning a rhythm of "listening forward" by setting aside regular times to just listen to God? Start by setting aside twenty to thirty minutes each week at a time that consistently works for you.

EAT

If you are not yet having a regular "family dinner night" with your own family, start by getting everyone to schedule at least one meal together each week.

When eating meals with your family or friends, reflect on and discuss how those times, those meals, are a picture of the gospel and Jesus' life given for us.

Ask God to show you two or three people or couples he would have you invite over for dinner in the next several weeks. Then, in faith, call and invite them!

IDENTITY AND RHYTHMS DIAGNOSTIC

BLESS

Spend some time making a mental list (or a written one) of all the things and people that God has blessed you with. Then take time to thank him for each of these. It may take a while!

Ask God what specific resources, skills, or abilities he has given you that he desires to bless others with. Then ask him who and when and how.

Pray for one of these opportunities to take place this week. Then go after another next week. Begin to live in a rhythm of blessing!

CELEBRATE

At the next birthday party, graduation, or wedding you attend, spend a few minutes reflecting on God's goodness in these people's lives and the ways this celebration is a reflection of God's heart and character.

Get together with a few close friends and plan a simple evening or holiday party, inviting several of your not-yet-believing friends. Your goal is to show God's extravagant, generous heart to one another through the food and drinks you serve. Make God's generosity to you your personal "theme" for the night.

What rhythms of celebration are going on in your city right now? Pray and ask God to lead you to participate regularly in one of these as his family's representative.

RE-CREATE

Set aside a time this week to read Hebrews 4:1 – 13. Meditate on the passage awhile, asking God to reveal his heart through his Word. Do you see any parallels to your own life?

What are the most restful, restorative things you do? How often do you do them? Is God the focus of these times? Can he be?

Look for a ten- to fifteen-minute part of your average day that you can set aside to rest and re-create your heart before God. You may need to schedule it in order to make it happen!

Ask God to show you a time this week that you can be with him resting, listening — enjoying. Try and set aside at least an hour for this. Look for ways to do this again next week, establishing a pattern of re-creation.

A FEW RESOURCES YOU MAY FIND HELPFUL

The Story-Formed Way. A ten-week journey through the entire Story of God for a community of disciples making disciples. http://www.gcmcollective.org/article/story-formed-way/

Story Training. Video training on how to lead a group through the Story of God effectively. http://www.gcmcollective.org/story-training/

Free Training Curriculum to follow along. http://www.gcmcollective.org/mediafiles/story-of-god-training.pdf

GCM Collective. A community of thousands all over the world who are beginning to live out their new identity in all of life and helping one another along the way. Many resources are available to you here to begin to form gospel communities living on mission. http://www.gcmcollective.org/

Stay connected to the author online via Twitter: @CaesarKal and on the web at caesarkalinowski.com

NOTES

CHAPTER 1

1. Acts 2:42–47.
2. See Matthew 19:16–21.
3. Some of the phrases and concepts in the book arose out of work done with Soma Communities and in conversations with Jeff Vanderstelt and others. The phrase "Family of Missionary Servants sent as disciples who make disciples" is an example of language we developed at Soma to express concepts contained in this book and to define our missional communities. I am grateful to Soma and its member for these insights.
4. You will notice throughout this book that I often refer to God as "Dad." Jesus referred to and called God "Father," *his* Father or *our* Father. Right before he went to the cross, when he was praying in a garden, Jesus cried, "*Abba,* Father" (Mark 14:36). The apostle Paul tells us in Romans 8:15, "The Spirit you received does not make you slaves, so that you live in fear again; rather, the Spirit you received brought about your adoption to sonship. And by him we cry, '*Abba,* Father.' *Abba* is the Aramaic word for Father, but it carries with it a tender, intimate, and warm sense. It has been most closely likened to our more modern use of the word *Daddy* or *Dad.* That's the feeling I want to have when I talk to God or think of him. He's my heavenly Daddy.
5. Hebrews 2:11.
6. Matthew 20:27–28.
7. John 13:16.
8. John 20:21–22.
9. Genesis 3:8–9.
10. See Genesis 1:26.

CHAPTER 2

1. This quote comes from a powerful book, *The Cure: What If God Isn't Who You Think He Is and Neither Are You,* by Bruce McNicol, Bill Thrall, and

NOTES

John Lynch (San Clemente, CA: CrossSection, 2012), Kindle ed., loc. 658. My heart and many of the thoughts I now hold, and share here, have been deeply shaped by the authors' work. I highly recommend reading this book. Twice.

2. Ibid.
3. Romans 8:20–22; 1 Corinthians 1:30.
4. John 15:9.
5. Ibid., loc. 623.
6. 2 Corinthians 1:21–22 NLT.
7. Romans 8:11 NLT.
8. Isaiah 64:6.
9. Right before Jesus left to return to heaven and sit at the right hand of his Father, he gave his disciples two commands: "Go and make disciples of mine all over the world" (Matt. 28:19, my paraphrase), and "First wait for the Holy Spirit which I am going to send to indwell you, leading you in all of the ways of wisdom and reminding you of everything I have taught you" (John 14:26). Then we read in Acts 2 that as the disciples gathered together in prayer, waiting to go out on Jesus' mission, something like a giant windstorm came and filled the room they were in and "All of them were filled with the Holy Spirit" (v. 4). Have you ever noticed that throughout the New Testament and in super-obvious ways in the book of Acts, the believers do almost nothing without getting their marching orders first from the Holy Spirit? The Spirit counseled them in church matters (Acts 15:28). The Spirit told them where and when to "preach" to people about Jesus (Acts 16:6–7). The Spirit filled the words they spoke with power (1 Thess. 1:4–8). The Spirit told them where to come and go on mission (Acts 20:22). The Spirit warned them of potential dangers (Acts 20:23). The Spirit helped them know how and what to pray (Rom. 8:26). I could keep going here, but you get the picture.
10. McNicol et al., The Cure, loc. 731.
11. James 2:14–17 NLT.
12. Luke 7:22.

CHAPTER 3

1. Francis Chan and Danae Yankoski, Crazy Love: Overwhelmed by a Relentless God (Colorado Springs: David C. Cook, 2008), Kindle ed., locs. 397–98.
2. Proverbs 22:6.
3. 1 Corinthians 12:14, 21–22, 24.
4. Matthew 25:35–36, 40.

CHAPTER 4

1. John 20:21–22.
2. John 17:15.
3. Matthew 23:25–26.
4. Jesus was given two names at the time of his birth: Jesus, meaning "the Lord who saves," and Emmanuel, which means, "God is with us." These two

names show us much of the reason Jesus came to this earth: He came to be with us, among us. And he came for our salvation — he is for us, on our side. We now live in the same way *with* and *for* others.

CHAPTER 5
1. Matthew 20:28.
2. John 13:16.
3. John 15:20.
4. Matthew 25:40.

CHAPTER 6
1. 1 Corinthians 8:1.
2. Ray Vander Laan, "In the Dust of the Rabbi," Vol. 6 in Faith Lessons Series (Grand Rapids: Zondervan, 2006).
3. John 15:16.
4. Matthew 28:19.
5. John 8:31 – 32.
6. Colossians 2:6 – 7.
7. Isaiah 49:15 – 16.
8. Romans 5:6 – 8.
9. Isaiah 51:1 – 2.

INTRODUCTORY MATERIAL FOR PART 3
1. I got this phrase, "moving from additional to intentional," from my friend and fellow missionary Alex Absalom while discussing life as a missionary. It has been a very helpful way to look at this concept.
2. Ephesians 5:15 – 16.
3. The six rhythms (story-formed, listen, eat, bless, celebrate, and re-create) is another set of ideas that arose from mine and others' work with Soma Communities, for which I am thankful.

CHAPTER 7
1. Hebrews 10:25.
2. Acts 2:42 – 47.
3. Dan Allender, *To Be Told: God Invites You to Coauthor Your Future* (Colorado Springs: WaterBrook, 2006), 11.
4. Galatians 4:9 NLT.
5. See John 4:1 – 42.
6. Chris Kinsley and Drew Francis, "A Woman of No Distinction," 2007, http://virtualmethodist.blogspot.com/2010/10/woman-of-no-distinction.html.
7. John 5:39 – 40 MSG.

CHAPTER 8
1. John 8:28 – 29.
2. Matthew 28:18 – 20.
3. See Genesis 2:16 – 17.
4. Proverbs 2:1 – 5 NLT.

5. John 16:12–13.
6. To check out some of what the Holy Spirit does in our lives, see John 14:15–20, 26; 15:26; 16:7–15; Romans 8:5–14; 1 Corinthians 2:10–14; and Galatians 5:16–26.

CHAPTER 9

1. Mark 10:45.
2. Luke 19:10.
3. Luke 7:34.
4. Tim Chester, *A Meal with Jesus: Discovering Grace, Community, and Mission around the Table (Re:Lit)* (Wheaton, IL: Crossway, 2011), 12, Kindle ed.
5. Luke 7:34.
6. Chester, *A Meal with Jesus*, 14.
7. Peter Leithart, *Blessed Are the Hungry: Meditations on the Lord's Supper* (Moscow, ID: Canon, 2000), 115.

CHAPTER 10

1. 2 Corinthians 9:8–9, 12.
2. 2 Corinthians 4:5–7 NLT.
3. A. B. Simpson, *A Larger Christian Life* (New York: Christian Alliance, 1890), 92–94.

CHAPTER 11

1. 1 Corinthians 10:30–31.
2. 1 Corinthians 16:13–14.
3. Matthew 26:29.

CHAPTER 12

1. Genesis 2:2–3.
2. Exodus 20:8.
3. John 15:5.

CHAPTER 13

1. Matthew 19:39.
2. Ephesians 6:12, italics added by author.
3. 1 Peter 5:8.
4. Neil Cole, *Organic Church: Growing Faith Where Life Happens* (San Francisco: Jossey-Bass, 2005), 72.

The Gospel Primer
An eight-week guide to transformation in community

by Caesar Kalinowski

The Gospel Primer by Caesar Kalinowski will help you creatively answer the question: *What is the Gospel?*

The primer examines the Story of God as found in scripture and teaches the reader to form a personal Gospel Story in a natural, yet powerful way. *The Gospel Primer* is designed to help any group of people cultivate a practical understanding of the Gospel and grow in Gospel fluency—the ability to proclaim and demonstrate the Gospel in every area of life. This unique resource will help you gain a deep understanding and practice of the Gospel.

Available from missiopublishing.com

Share Your Thoughts

With the Author: Your comments will be forwarded to the author when you send them to *zauthor@zondervan.com*.

With Zondervan: Submit your review of this book by writing to *zreview@zondervan.com*.

Free Online Resources at
www.zondervan.com

Daily Bible Verses and Devotions: Enrich your life with daily Bible verses or devotions that help you start every morning focused on God. Visit www.zondervan.com/newsletters.

Free Email Publications: Sign up for newsletters on Christian living, academic resources, church ministry, fiction, children's resources, and more. Visit www.zondervan.com/newsletters.

Zondervan Bible Search: Find and compare Bible passages in a variety of translations at www.zondervanbiblesearch.com.

Other Benefits: Register to receive online benefits like coupons and special offers, or to participate in research.